Praise for *Tarot Tableau Revolution*

"With her clear and genuine writing, María Alviz Hernando's *Tarot Tableau Revolution* will assist new readers to build a great foundation for their tarot journeys, while it will help experienced readers find a solid way to interpret fine details that are vital for good readings and to provide a direct route to answer questions at hand."

—Kristine Gorman, creator of *Visionary Woman Tarot*

"The first time I learned the nine-card tableau method from María was in a class a few years ago. After only an hour of practicing this method, I just knew it would become my preferred reading style—and I was right. Now, I hold her book, *Tarot Tableau Revolution,* in my hands, and it has unlocked layers of subtlety in the cards, enhancing readings not just for me but for the benefit of others. The tableau method is a versatile skill that all tarot practitioners should know about."

—Stacey Williams-Ng, author of *The Southern Gothic Oracle Trilogy* and *Rhythm and Soul Tarot*

"Rooted in respect for tarot's deep symbolism, yet unafraid to challenge convention, *Tarot Tableau Revolution* brings a fresh, authentic voice to modern divination."

—Erika Robinson, author of *The Language of Lenormand*

"More than a tarot book, *Tarot Tableau Revolution* is a homecoming for anyone who's ever felt outside the frame. María Alviz Hernando writes with heart and precision, reminding us that revolution can be gentle, joyful, and deeply personal."

—Nancy Hendrickson, author of *Ancestral Tarot*

"The tarot is, before all, about storytelling, and *Tarot Tableau Revolution* is a practical and insightful guide that helps you attain that objective. This comprehensive book teaches you the art of tableau reading, starting with how to place the cards, the basic techniques, and how to progressively tell a story by roaming among all the rows and columns. Whether you're a beginner, intermediate or seasoned reader, *Tarot Tableau Revolution* has step-by-step examples and exercises to help you become more fluent in complex readings and situations. A must-read for practitioners at all levels who want to improve their skills in reading and telling stories with tarot."

—Serge Pirotte, author of *The Art of Interpreting Lenormand* and *Mastering the Oracle Belline*

"An inspirational teacher and visionary in the world of divination, María Alviz Hernando's heartfelt love for the tarot overflows in her brilliant book, *Tarot Tableau Revolution.* Filled with insightful interpretations and spread demonstrations, the book highlights María's wise tutoring that can empower your confidence to read the symbolic messages within the cards. A powerful resource, her work offers a secure means to uncover your tarot path to success."

—Kooch N. Daniels, author of *Stars, Cards, and Stones* and *Tarot D'Amour*

"María Alviz Hernando's strong and capable voice is ushering in a new generation of tarot wisdom. Her techniques and guidance offer us fundamental skills for modern tarot, as well as the understanding to discover the depth and nuance the cards hold for us."

—Christiana Gaudet, author of *Fortune Stellar* and *Tarot Tour Guide*

"I've been practicing tarot for over thirty years and feel utterly refreshed by *Tarot Tableau Revolution.* María Alviz Hernando gives the tableau its due, giving this wonderful intuitive technique the loving attention it deserves. Her writing is warm and encouraging—it's like having a conversation with a very smart friend who genuinely wants to help you succeed. Alviz patiently unpacks this simple way of letting the cards speak to each other, breaking the process down into clear, manageable steps that feel both easy and surprisingly nuanced. I've had a lot of off-and-on over the years with positional spreads and haven't always felt a comfortable 'click' with the most common ones, like the Celtic Cross. But with *Tarot Tableau Revolution,* I found myself saying 'oh, yes, of course, that makes perfect sense' each time I picked it up. This book is a real gift for anyone who's ever felt frustrated with finding the right spread or wanted a more flowing approach to their readings. The technique works, and María's gentle guidance makes it almost effortless to learn."

—Elizabeth Russell, creator of the Dreamfruit series

"While I am a neuroscientist, I tend to have fanciful ways of explaining the art of tarot and sometimes struggle to make it relevant and practical. I always thought it was because it is an esoteric practice, with the mysticism making it more abstract and difficult to explain. With *Tarot Tableau Revolution*, María Alviz Hernando has shown me how one can be both intuitive and insightful while being efficient, practical, and, dare I say, clinical. She is able to lay out the cards, their correspondences, and interactions with such precision that learning becomes easier and gives one the tools to move towards mastery. I love that there is no wishy-washy aspect of the interpretation of 'Oh, it is up to you to decide what it means'—but a clear explanation as to why different symbology can be interpreted a certain way. María is also not shy about stating right at the beginning that it is important for a reader to answer questions directly. This straightforward nature that María lays out in the beginning is the throughline in the entire book—what you see is what you get, and you get layers and layers of information that you can add to your tarot toolkit. Part 2 of the book was eye opening for me, as I do not use the tableau system. Folks have tried to explain this to me many times, but it kind of just went over my head. But here María holds your hand through the process, offering different ways to approach the tableau. Her personal examples and insights really help one to navigate the tarot tableau. Questions are again highlighted in the last segment of the book where she delves into the importance of the question and then offers tangible ways for you to read for relationships, finances, career, health, and spiritual growth. The specificity and focus with which she interprets the cards is fantastic!

If you are looking for a way to jumpstart your tarot readings toward focused answering of questions, rather than just dabbling with vagaries, I would suggest that you pick this book up! María sets the mood and ambience of the room by giving the flavor of each card, then sets the table and the menu by providing structure with the tableau, and then proceeds to deliver a feast of answering queries with the final section. You will come away with practical tools, straightforward answers to doubts, and a wealth of knowledge."

—Siddharth Ramakrishnan, PhD, author of *The Neuroscience of Tarot*

Tarot Tableau Revolution

Tarot Tableau Revolution

A Breakthrough System to See the Whole Story in Your Readings

MARÍA ALVIZ HERNANDO

foreword by MARY K. GREER

WEISER BOOKS

This edition first published in 2025 by Weiser Books, an imprint of
Red Wheel/Weiser, LLC
With offices at:
65 Parker Street, Suite 7
Newburyport, MA 01950
www.redwheelweiser.com

ISBN: 978-1-57863-884-0
Library of Congress Cataloging-in-Publication Data
Names: Hernando, Maria Alviz, 1992- author | Greer, Mary K. (Mary Katherine) writer of foreword Title: Tarot tableau revolution : a breakthrough system to see the whole story in your readings / Maria Alviz Hernando ; foreword by Mary K. Greer. Description: Newburyport, MA : Weiser Books, 2025. | Summary: "Among the very earliest methods of divining with tarot cards involved the tableau. The technique involves laying out cards in a square or rectangular shape and interpreting them like one might interpret a painting. Cards are read in relationship to one another. This book brings this method to a modern audience, offering tips and techniques for mastery of the system and teaching people to read tarot based on classic cartomantic techniques. Readers learn how the cards interact on different levels: elemental, directional, relational. This way, they can easily commit to a concrete answer in their readings, as the multiple elements allow them to substantiate their interpretation"-- Provided by publisher.
Identifiers: LCCN 2025017715 | ISBN 9781578638840 trade paperback | ISBN 9781633413764 ebook Subjects: LCSH: Tarot | Tarot cards | BISAC: BODY, MIND & SPIRIT / Divination / Tarot | BODY, MIND & SPIRIT / Divination / Fortune Telling Classification: LCC BF1879.T2 H4525 2025 | DDC 133.3/2424--dc23/eng/20250805 LC record available at https://lccn.loc.gov/2025017715

Cover art and interior design by Sky Peck Design
Interior card images from the *Weiser Tarot* © RedWheel/Weiser
Typeset in Arno Pro

Printed in the United States of America
IBI

10 9 8 7 6 5 4 3 2 1

To Pedro, Toni, and Leslie.
None of this would have happened without you.
I love you.

Contents

Foreword

Tarot has been a major part of my life since 1967, resulting in the writing of many books on personal insight tarot techniques. Yet over the years, I've expanded my divinatory skills and continued to stretch my abilities by learning to read with classic cartomancy decks, primarily Lenormand and regular playing cards. I've managed to find lost objects, decide what meal to order at a restaurant, and guide clients through difficult relationships. The cartomantic systems offer precise, grounded information, often where more symbolic or therapeutic methods might wander or hesitate.

In my explorations, I noticed that the 19th-century magical order from which many modern tarot decks descend—the Hermetic Order of the Golden Dawn—borrowed heavily from earlier cartomancy traditions. These include the use of significators, card-counting techniques, consistent and limited core meanings, and large layouts. Interpretation in these systems relies less on intuition or archetype and more on following basic rules of proximity, position, and pattern—structure over symbol.

Since the mid-20th century tarot reading has expanded well beyond revealing things: the unknown (*How does he feel about me?*), advice (*What will help me get a raise? or Which option is better?*), or prediction (*Will I get the job?*). Modern tarot readings often call on mythic wisdom and psycho-spiritual guidance but also delve into early, even past-life or ancestral trauma; encourage dialogue with tarot-personified Shadow figures; or petition a tarot archetype to reveal your deepest soul-purpose. In place of clear answers, these readings provide complex layers of insight through metaphorical storytelling, shining light on the darkest corners of your dilemma but often failing to give clear, actionable direction.

Maria Alviz Hernando, an experienced, knowledgeable, and highly regarded card reader and teacher, is here to help you. What makes María's approach so effective is that she brings to tarot what is often missing from traditional instruction and lacking in tarot books and classes: precision, proximity, directionality, and tableau.

So, what if you're truly drawn to tarot? Perhaps you have a favorite deck whose images speak to you or one that keeps whispering, "pick me." When reading tableau, María demonstrates that tarot will work as well or better than those other kinds of decks. I often use a small, fluorescent pink Rider-Waite-Smith style tarot for this kind of work—perfect for large layouts and surprisingly insistent in its simplicity, while still preserving the tarot patterning of repeating images, elements, courts, and numbering.

While modern readers are often encouraged to simply "go with their intuition," María offers tools that sharpen intuition. In traditional tarot spreads where cards are isolated in separate positions, a card showing someone sadly bent over fallen cups could be seen by one reader as saying it's time to move on: Stop crying over spilt milk. Whereas another reader might insist that the Five of Cups is about acknowledging your sorrow and not rushing things, María shows how specific cues, through adjacency and structure, can guide the reader toward the most likely interpretation.

Several years ago, I wrote a series of blog posts about using both Lenormand and tarot cards to explore a movie, play, or song. I mostly used Lenormand to describe the plot, story line, and basic intent—either as prediction before or summary afterward. They best describe clues as to what's happening, to whom, and the major crisis points. Afterwards I used tarot to explore the theme and deeper meanings or to reflect and process my own emotional reactions. With tarot you can reflect on multiple layers revealing what the story signifies or feels like. In Maria's big-picture tarot readings, the story and how it is likely to play out emerges from the adjacency of cards and the flow among them. By using tarot in these tableau formations, meaning still emerges as an inner play and the interplay among needs, soul perspectives, and life lessons.

Patterns that emerge in even the largest of these tableaus can be as intuitive as they are reliable, benefiting from objectivity, a clear eye, and attention to detail. The rules may seem intricate at first but quickly become second nature and kind of fun—"knighting" is one of my favorite techniques. Rewards pour in when you discover how practical these methods are, how clear the information can be, and how well they work for delivering advice and recommendations that can be substantiated.

Personally, I still want to peek at what's under the tablecloth in the Nine of Cups. While others will be more pleased to know that the figure in that happy card is surrounded by all the methods he found in this book that will help both reader and client feel more secure, more seen, and better prepared.

No matter what kind of tarot reader you are, the skills you learn here will become a valuable part of your practice.

—Mary K. Greer,
author of *Archetypal Tarot: What Your Birth Card Reveals About Your Personality, Your Path, and Your Potential*

Acknowledgments

In hindsight, the road to publishing this book has been woven by a million beautiful little happenings: choices, plot twists, interventions, apparent detours that in the end were actually leading to the right place, and, above all, a lot of people—as well as some luck. Well, a lot of luck, actually.

At risk of sounding like an Oscar's acceptance speech, I would like to thank my parents for taking it like absolute champs when I said that I wanted to be a tarot reader for a living. If they were disappointed, I never knew. Also, thank you for insisting on making me learn English when I didn't want to. It didn't go down as you expected, but at least you got your money's worth in that regard.

I want to thank my husband, Pedro, for his unwavering support and his faith in me, and for being the most amazing, loving partner (and a prolific funder of tarot decks). My life and my deck collection wouldn't be as rich without you. Toni, for everything that she has done and continues to do, proving herself time and again to be the best friend I could ask for. Leslie, my very first and most extraordinary "padawan," now dear friend, to whom I owe the very foundation of this book. This is dedicated to the three of you.

Christiana, for being an inspiration and a friend. You will never know to what extent you have influenced me to get here.

Jane, Kamille, Marion, Niamh, Ana, you have been cheerleaders, trouble-shooters, and a safe haven in this and all things. Thank you endlessly.

Sonoma and Liam, you're an absolute privilege to teach and an even greater privilege to know.

A huge thank you to my editor, Judika Illes, for holding my hand through this entire process and for having my back. I wasn't sure what to expect but surely you have exceeded every expectation. To Laurie for her warmth, kindness, and support. And to Bobbi, whose friendship never decays.

Lastly, a thank you to all of those that, in one way or another, have contributed to this journey, especially the ones who laid the foundation stone: Fran, J., Natalia, and of course my dad, who bought that very first pendulum without hesitation.

Introduction

I like to think of this book as the book I would have liked to read when I picked up my first deck of cards at the age of fourteen, when I had no idea what I was doing. I remember having so many questions and only one little booklet in which I could find answers. I would pull cards (three cards in a past—present—future layout because it was the only layout I knew) for whoever would let me, using the Major Arcana only because that's what I had been told to do. I felt the kind of excitement that makes the tips of your fingers tickle as I began to pull my first cards, of which I understood very little.

I believe I was lucky to be at that age where you wildly overestimate your own knowledge, when you have the confidence to be wrong out loud without so much as blushing. Had I taken an interest in tarot later, my story might have been different. I took what little I knew and ran fearlessly, practicing, practicing, and practicing. The cards helped me navigate the turmoil of my full-steam teenage angst, which included questionable romantic choices (and the ever-present question, which I asked more times than I would like to admit: "Will he come back?"), episodes of high school bullying (I'm probably not the only weird kid around, right?), and the early stages of a spiritual path that was not at all common in my environment.

I probably didn't make the best or even the healthiest use of tarot in my early stages as a practitioner, but that relentless practice made me come to know and integrate the cards into my life in a significant way. Years went by and my confidence began to fade. For a period of time I barely touched my cards, a result of a crisis of faith that had more to do with poor choices and the belief that the divine was the equivalent of a magic lamp than with any real doubt. That story would probably be better suited for a memoir tentatively titled *My Poor Life Choices*. My cards remained an afterthought until I was introduced to a guy who would later become my friend—and then later, *not* my friend—who was, and I guess is, a brilliant card reader. Through our practice together, I reconnected with my love for tarot, though not yet with my confidence.

A couple of years into our friendship, we began toying with the idea of reading tarot together professionally. At that point I had been reading for eight-ish years, but the bold confidence of my beginnings was long gone. It was this person who introduced me to a way of traditional reading he had learned. This method of reading involved some of the basics that I later developed into what would become the contents of this book. He showed me two layouts. The first involved the use of all the Major Arcana cards in a configuration of three rows of seven cards each, plus one at the end of the middle row. The second was a layout of twelve cards in four rows of three that inspired within me the idea for the Nine Card Tableau. I would later discover that the Nine Card Tableau was not entirely my idea, but instead a way of reading that had existed for centuries.

These two spreads were pivotal to my development as a reader. They gave me enough confidence to begin to read for the public. Ironically, these matters of confidence on the one hand and trust on the other were what caused a fracture in that friendship. Even so, I will be forever grateful to this person for what he taught me, as well as for everything that transpired later that forced me to manage on my own. I would probably not be writing this had things gone differently, so thank you, J, wherever you are. Truly.

What you are about to discover in these pages is a reading system that will revolutionize your reading style and serve as a foundation upon which you will be able to build solid interpretations for every question: the tableau system. Once you've learned it, you'll be able to fill in the gaps in your reading that adding correspondences on top of correspondences never seemed to fill. You will move from card-by-card interpretation to having a full view of your spreads. This approach may appear intricate and intimidating at first, but by reading this book, you'll learn to build upon the information presented, starting from simple narrative reading in lines of three to five cards, and growing into the Nine Card Tableau, the most versatile spread to ever exist. Eventually, you'll be able to read a 5x5 Tableau or a Major Arcana or Grand Tableau with ease. (The Major Arcana Tableau and the Grand Tableau are two different methods of reading the same tableau.)

At this stage, you probably have many questions. Number one: What is the tableau system?

Let's start from the beginning. *Tableau* is French for "canvas" or "picture." This means two things when it comes to our readings: one, that our layouts are going to be in a square or box shape, just like a canvas, and two, that our cards paint a picture. This picture is composed of many layers, strokes, colors, techniques, and details. The finished scene, the painting, is the last step. To get there, to our final interpretation of the scene we're being shown, we will travel through different layers: situating our reading in time in accordance to the question asked or the situation of the querent; analyzing the elements both present and absent in the spread and how they affect the question; understanding the core of the matter; and identifying the factors that are affecting the situation from the outside, as well as the areas in which the querent can effect change through their actions, leading ultimately to an outcome. After blending all these factors together, we will be able to divine the full story.

If you are even somewhat familiar with cartomancy, chances are that you have heard the term tableau before, perhaps in the context of Lenormand. Lenormand is another system of cartomancy utilizing a deck of thirty-six cards. Its origin is debated to be French or German, and while it is often attributed to Marie Anne Lenormand, a popular French cartomancer who lived during the Napoleonic era, it is possible that such attribution is more marketing than reality. Regardless, this is a system that employs numerous cartomantic techniques, among which is the tableau. Is the tableau system a Lenormand thing? Well, yes and no. Tableau reading doesn't belong to Lenormand any more than hammers belong to blacksmiths. Tableau reading is used in Lenormand, but it is not exclusive to Lenormand, even if Lenormand gained the tableau system popularity. The tableau is a cartomantic technique that can be applied to any system: Tarot, Lenormand, Kipper, Belline, La Vera Sibilla Italiana, or any other card-based divinatory system.

The system that I use is the result of combining several methods together, yet I cannot say that it is exclusively my creation. The tableau system has existed since early in the history of cartomancy as one of its most common divinatory methods. To attest to this, you can see evidence of a squared disposition of cards in several paintings and engravings that include themes of fortune-telling and cartomancy. The examples shown on pages 4 and 5 date back as early as the mid-18th century.

Every reader at every stage of their development can use tableau. It doesn't matter whether you got your first deck last week or have lived through five different popes with a deck in your hands. If you are new to tarot, first, congratulations on your new journey and my condolences to your wallet. Second, incorporating tableau into your journey early on will probably save you from so many headaches. While this is not a book of meanings—refer to the back of this book for my recommended reading—it provides a way of reading that will facilitate your learning.

"Fortune Teller" George Morland (1763–1804) Tate Modern Gallery

"Fortune Teller" Harry Herman Roseland (1867–1950)

"The Fortune Teller" Mikhail Ivanovich Skotti (1814–1861)

The techniques described in this book will help you integrate both the external and the internal factors in the reading, resulting in a well-rounded, practical, and relevant interpretation that will offer you or your querents practical insights.

What are those factors and how do they affect the reading? Every circumstance that brings a querent to our table is unique and should be treated as such. A pull of cards in the context of a fresh romantic connection should be interpreted in a vastly different way from the cards in the context of a querent who is wondering if they should consider a job offer in a different country. The external factors that play an important role in determining our situation are the following.

The Question: It is essential to know the topic of our reading, even if there is no evident question—which doesn't mean there isn't a question at all! This is the first step toward identifying the lens through which we approach the reading and build our interpretation.

The Context: The context or background of the question also gives us a hint as to what to look for in a reading—and thus, facilitates its interpretation. For example, it's not the same thing to read for a new or potential relationship as it is to read for an established one, or with a relationship that is rocky versus one that is dulled. A self-employed querent may have different concerns from one that is employed by a company, even if both want to inquire about their careers.

The Method: Each divinatory system that we use to perform our reading has its particular set of rules. We don't read Marseilles tarot in the same way that we read tarot in a Rider Waite Smith fashion, and of course we don't read, for instance, Belline with the same set of rules that we read tarot. Our method of choice will make the reading present in a particular way that is unique to it.

The Spread: The layout that we choose to interpret the message and how it applies to the matter at hand plays an important role. Whether you go with a positional spread (such as the Horseshoe or the Celtic Cross) or, in the case of tableau, you choose a Nine Card Tableau or a 5x5 matters. After reading this book, I'm confident you will probably never have a problem choosing a spread ever again!

Among the internal factors of the reading, which we will elaborate upon later on in this book, we can count all matters that have to do with the cards that are, or are not, on the table.

Elemental Configuration: The elemental configuration refers to the suits that are present or absent in the reading, and their effect on the question and context of the matter at hand. The elemental configuration of the spread will give us a lot of information in our reading.

Imagery and Directionality: The visual cues and patterns, as well as the symbolism, directions, and body language of the characters in the cards, add a valuable layer of information about the energy and attitudes in the situation, as well as the interactive patterns.

Numbers and Numeric Patterns: The numeric interaction in the spread can give hints as to the stage in which the situation is, as well as add insight as to the development of it.

Traditional Card Meanings: This layer is composed of the traditional meanings of the cards, along with our other layers of interpretation.

Intuitive Insights: This includes the psychic or intuitive response of the reader to all the above.

The combination of the above internal and external reading factors and the cartomantic techniques that we will discover are the strokes and layers that compose our final interpretation: the picture that is the tableau.

Finally, I would like to offer some insight into my approach to tarot and what I believe a reading should be. These are the principles that I work with, but they don't have to be the ones you live by; however, these insights will help you better understand my approach to reading. The great thing about tableau reading is that it's very versatile and adaptable, so even if your approach to tarot is different from my own, you will still be able to adapt tableau reading to whatever works best for you.

I believe in tarot as a predictive as well as an analytic tool. My stance is that prediction is a thing that we do in so many areas of our lives, and in so many fields. Climate specialists predict the weather, physicians predict the progression of an illness, economists predict the financial climate as well as the ups and downs of the market. Mothers predict that children are going to fall from that swing, land on their chins, and come to them crying. DNA testing predicts whether we are more likely to suffer an illness, and, in a less sophisticated way, our family history predicts what kinds of issues we will most likely experience with our bodies. We predict so many things in so many different ways that, to me, it doesn't make sense to deny the predictive nature of tarot.

Does that mean that we have no choice in any matter? Of course not! Storms pass by quicker than expected, not every dip in the economy turns into a crisis, everyone knows someone whose great auntie lived to 110 years old while smoking two packs a day, and having a particular gene doesn't mean that you will necessarily develop an illness. Still, the statistics are there for a reason.

Analysis comes hand-in-hand with prediction. We need to analyze the situation to be able to understand it. From how it came to be and why we are in this circumstance, to where we stand, what influences and options are available to us, and what the paths forward are, analysis is a powerful tool. Having a map is pretty pointless if we don't know where we are located!

I also believe that, aside from being predictive and analytic, a reading needs to be relevant and practical. What do I mean by relevant? If my querent comes to me with a concern about their job, there's no point in me instead reading about their love life. The reading needs to be relevant to their concern. Personally, I am not often one to reframe questions (although I will make some suggestions about what will get the best results) because I believe that everyone is entitled to their own concerns. Finally, a reading must be practical and understandable, interpreted in plain language that the querent can use and apply to their lives.

My readings are based on two principles. The first is that any question can be answered with tarot if you know what to look for. (Even the weirdest ones.) The second is that the reading is always about the question asked, and not something else. You could get three different stories from the same spread if you ask three different questions. That the same cards can tell different stories and that they must be interpreted in relation to the querent's concern, is in my opinion the job of a reader.

With that said, I'll give you one last piece of advice before we continue forward. When practicing the tableau, don't be too creative in the beginning. Use a deck with which you're already familiar. This will make it easier for you to spot patterns and themes, and to identify interactions without adding an extra layer of difficulty by diverting your attention into deciphering a new deck. My approach is based on the Rider Waite Smith deck, but you can easily translate this into the Marseilles tradition, the Thoth tradition, or use this with any other method of reading.

And now, at last, let's divine!

PART I

READING IN LAYERS

The First Steps to Tableau Reading

IF THE TABLEAU IS A PAINTING, then in this first part of the book we look at the elements of that composition. We are going to walk through each stroke of the brush that composes the painting and understand its role in the final work of art.

The strokes and layers of our tableau are the elements and suits both present and absent in our reading: the numbers, the colors, pictorial cues, the body language of the figures, directionality, interactions, relational dynamics, and, of course, the meanings of the cards.

This can be a lot to take in initially, which is why this reading method is layered.

What Is Layered Reading?

I'm a fan of allegories when it comes to explanations. To understand layered reading, we can think of the reading as a puzzle. This exercise was inspired by the puzzle of Monet's *The Japanese Footbridge* that hangs in my office.

When you're putting together a puzzle, the first step (unless you like to suffer) is usually separating and sorting the pieces. In your first pass, you separate the pieces that have a blunt edge in order to put together the frame. The frame serves as a structure upon which to build the rest. Then, you sort the pieces by color so that you can guesstimate where they fit. Once you've done that, you put the border together.

If we refer back to *The Japanese Footbridge*, it makes sense to then separate the pieces into a few categories. You would have a pile for the green pieces that form the background, a pile for the pieces that show a bit of bridge, a pile of pinkish pieces that form the waterlilies, a pile for the reeds, and a pile for the water.

Once you've done that, you would naturally begin trying to attach the pieces to the border. Maybe you would like to start with the bridge to help you divide the puzzle into two distinguishable portions, and then attach the pieces to the background and the water, and so on and so forth until your puzzle is complete.

This is exactly what we do when we are reading a tableau. First, we look at the cards on the table, account for them, and take a series of steps towards putting the story together. If a card is a piece of the puzzle, there's only so much that we can learn from it on its own. We instead understand the card by how it connects with others. Some pieces of the puzzle, like the corners, are easily identifiable on their own; they also connect only two other pieces (cards). The rest of the border pieces connect with three other pieces, while the ones in the middle are going to link four pieces together, one on each side. In the same fashion, the role of some cards in the reading will be evident from the first moment, but that won't separate them from their role in the rest of the reading. Ultimately we need all of them to truly interpret the image.

Instead of interpreting one card in one particular position one at a time and being done with it, tableau reading integrates all of the cards in the spread. They are not individual cards but part of something else, a bigger picture. These layers explore different aspects of the cards, a different side of the puzzle piece.

This style of reading requires repeatedly going through the cards until you are able to extract all the information. Don't worry if it seems like too much at first! It's easier than it seems. Accompany me through these pages and get ready to begin to separate the pieces of our puzzle, the strokes of our painting, and I promise you that you will not want to look back.

Chapter 1

Core Meanings

The concept of core meanings is one of the first things I teach my students, especially those who are new to tarot and just beginning to learn the meanings of the cards. I encourage you to read this chapter even if you are a seasoned reader who knows the card meanings by heart, as it may open up new perspectives.

If you are completely new to tarot, and you are still learning (or have not yet learned) any meanings, core meaning exercises can help facilitate the process for you. This chapter is oriented towards *understanding* the cards, as opposed to simply memorizing them. And yes, a level of memorization is required in order to read. (You won't catch me dead saying something like, "Throw away the guidebook! Read only intuitively!") However, truly understanding the cards goes much deeper than simple memorization.

This is a time-consuming system, but one that will not only help you truly understand each card, but also keep you from forgetting its meaning.

Start with a card, ideally The Fool, and do some reading about it. There are so many resources out there about card meanings, both online and in books. (See the Recommended Reading section at the end of this book for my recommended tarot reading!) The goal is to read about The Fool, paying special attention and absorbing what you can about the card. Take notes if you want, though at this point I find bullet points more useful instead of long paragraphs or pages upon pages of notes. You can even create your own tarot bullet journal.

When you feel you have gathered enough information on a single card, think about a single word, or a short concept, that sums up the essence of the card.

This word or concept would ideally be:

- As neutral as possible. Avoid words with connotations that are inherently positive or negative.

- One word if possible. If it's not, a concept summed up in two or three words.

What if you can't find a neutral word? That's okay. It's not always possible. Just try not to assign an absolute value to the card. If, for instance, you look at the Ten of Swords and your core meaning is "defeat," consider that while defeat can mean absolute devastation, it can also be what finally allows a soldier to come back home from the front. If you look at The Sun and your core meaning of choice is "joy," keep in mind that while joy can mean happiness, it doesn't necessarily mean that what you enjoy and what is good for you are the same thing.

Many would call this a keyword, and it could be in the sense that it "unlocks" the rest of the meanings in your head. The thing that makes this concept different from keyword learning is that you are not simply learning a handful of keywords per card and calling it a day. You are gathering information and summing it up into a word or concept that encompasses the meaning of the card.

Let's apply this method to The Fool together so you can see how it works, and how you can repeat this process with the rest of the cards.

If you research The Fool, you will find information about the number assigned to the card, zero, and how it is a symbol of full potential. You will read about the symbolism in the card: the careless attitude of the young man approaching a cliff, indicating his openness and willingness to fall into the unknown. Consider the small dog that seems to bark and chase after him: Is he trying to warn him of impending danger, or is he a faithful companion? You will read about the light baggage that he carries over his shoulder, and how he doesn't need much, nor does he preserve a lot either. The white rose in his hand represents his innocence, and so on and so forth. You will come across the famous Fool's Journey, a metaphor for the journey through life, and read a myriad of different interpretations that add up on each other.

You may even find resources that analyze every color and symbol contained in the card. Other resources will give you a few keywords. Here are a few, for example: beginnings, innocence, freedom, adventure, spontaneity, recklessness, inexperience.

Once you have gone through all that information and hopefully taken some notes, it's time to think about what all of these things have in common. This is a way to narrow the card down to a single word or concept that unlocks the rest of the information.

Let's write down some bullet points about The Fool.

- He's young.
- He's innocent/inexperienced/reckless.
- He's adventurous.
- He represents beginnings.
- He doesn't carry heavy baggage.

To me, there is a clear word, my core meaning, that defines both the positive and negative traits of The Fool, and it is "new."

"New" as a concept applies to a beginning, to youth, to lack of experience, to innocence, to adventure, to freedom to act as one pleases. It is also something that is not yet established. While The Fool can herald a beginning, a new adventure, opportunity, or even a new romance, there are no guarantees about its durability. Even the worst traits of The Fool, such as unpredictability or recklessness, tie into the concept of "new" in some way. Someone who behaves in an unpredictable way can show a side of themselves that has not been seen before. Recklessness comes from naiveté and a lack of exposure to consequences, which in the end leads back to a lack of experience and, therefore, to the concept of "new."

This doesn't mean that "new" is all that The Fool represents, but that, with that core meaning in place, it is easier to unlock the multiple possibilities of the card.

Your core meaning may not be the same as mine and that is perfectly okay! I have even changed some of my core meanings as I have evolved as a reader. I have done an exercise with multiple students in which we exchanged our core meanings and we often found out that the other person had a point we hadn't considered. I have adopted core meanings from my students that I found better than my original, and vice versa. Alternatively, I may have learned a new word that I found perfectly fitting to the essence of the card!

You don't need to set these core meanings in stone. They can evolve with you as you grow as a reader. Your core meanings also don't have to look like anyone else's. (I mean, if your core meaning for The Tower is "party," then maybe I would like to have a talk with you.) The only thing that you need to keep in mind for your core meanings is that they are based on understanding the cards and not on memorization.

Expanding Your Card Meanings

Now that you have worked with your core meanings, it may be time to expand on those meanings. This is when you begin to look at the card in different contexts.

The meaning of a standalone card can take you only so far unless it is blended with the rest of the cards on the table. That being said, considering individual cards in different contexts can help widen your perspective and put you in a position of interpretative advantage. Expanding your card meanings grants you the grace to not stop and wonder, for example, what the Ten of Cups, a card traditionally associated with relationships, is doing in a career reading.

To do this, interrogate your card. Think about all the information you have learned about it, the paths that lead to your core meaning. Ask your card questions to help you expand your views.

Here is a list of questions that you can ask and answer with your card. Make a point to answer each question with the card so that you can see it working in different environments. I've drawn a card at random to go through this list of questions with you so I can give you an example of how you can find an answer to each question.

I'm doing this exercise with the Nine of Swords.

Q: What behaviors does this card support?

A: Caffeine consumption. Staying awake. Pondering our fears against reality. Being a night owl.

Q: What behaviors does this card warn against?

A: Insomnia. Remorse and regret. Being overly worried or fearful.

Q: How does this card describe personal strength?

A: Being in touch with one's fears and limitations without letting them take over. Heightened productivity and creativity at nighttime.

Q: How does this card describe personal weakness?

A: Over-thinking. A tendency to be disproportionately fearful. Going over one's perceived mistakes over and over again. Anxiety.

Q: How does this card describe an individual's personality?

A: Generally anxious, with a tendency to second-guess oneself. A worrier. A person with a tendency to anticipate trouble and poor outcomes.

Q: How does this card describe a day?

A: Exhausting, probably a day after a lousy night of sleep. Restless. A day with aches and pains.

Q: How does this card describe an established relationship?

A: A relationship with bed issues. They may not sleep together. They may not be able to rest while they are together. It is a relationship where at least one of the partners has concerns.

Q: How does this card describe a new relationship?

A: Likely to be a rebound relationship. Something used as a crutch to avoid thinking about painful stuff. A relationship where commitment is a concern. Unstable.

Q: How does this card describe a troubled relationship?

A: Walking on eggshells. A relationship in which one of the partners doesn't know where they stand. A relationship in which there's fear, either of a breakup or something else.

Q: How does this card describe a breakup?

A: This is a well-thought-out breakup that is the result of many sleepless nights. The reason for the breakup probably has to do with fears that were not put at ease throughout the relationship or other problems.

Q: How does this card describe a problem?

A: A concern, something that could go wrong but that has not manifested tangibly yet. "Did I close the door?" "Did I turn off the gas?" The perceived consequences of a situation that we fear.

Q: How does this card describe something that is broken?

A: Something that probably was not correctly put together. There's a missing piece, or something has been put in the incorrect place.

Q: How does this card describe an opportunity?

A: Scary, the kind of opportunity that makes one uncomfortable.

Q: How does this card describe academics?

A: Evening classes. Studying to become a sleep specialist. A medical specialization in issues pertaining to headaches and other ailments of the area.

Q: How does this card describe a profession/career?

A: Medical specializations that apply to sleep and head-related issues. Professions or careers that require night shifts.

Q: How does this card describe a working environment?

A: Highly demanding, with no time for rest. A very noisy environment with no personal space.

Q: How does this card describe a financial situation?

A: Dire enough to prevent good rest. Not knowing how to face the next day.

Q: How does this card describe a salary?

A: Lower than what's needed to make ends meet.

Q: How does this card describe an investment?

A: High risk. Very volatile. A bad investment.

Q: How does this card describe a purchase?

A: Late-night Amazon order. A purchase you would make while randomly scrolling through your phone, unable to sleep.

Q: How does this card describe a health issue?

A: Sleep issues. Sleep apnea. Migraine. Headaches. Insomnia.

Q: How does this card describe a solution?

A: The Nine of Swords tends to find a problem for every solution. This card suggests that the solution is there, past the worst-case scenario thinking, and is more obvious than it seems.

Q: How does this card describe a friend?

A: This card can speak of a somewhat needy friend with a tendency to worry and cause drama.

Q: How does this card describe an enemy?

A: The kind of enemy who constantly believes that one is plotting against them, and that they are righteous in defending themselves.

Q: How does this card describe a spiritual practice?

A: Spirituality of convenience, calling on the divine in times of worry or need only.

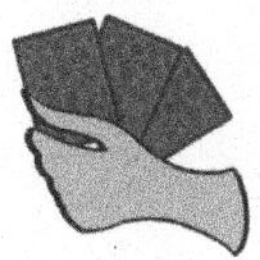

EXERCISE: Now it's your turn! Shuffle your deck and pick up a card, any card. (Yes, even Court Cards.) Do your best to go through the list and answer the questions to help you see this card in different contexts!

Chapter 2

The Elements

Let's delve into the elemental correspondences of the cards and their interactions to discover how they affect the reading. We'll explore the role of each element in different contexts and learn how to associate the elements with key aspects of each situation to fully understand them.

I aim to eliminate the simplification that Pentacles are always about money and Cups about feelings. This can be a foundation upon which you can develop a greater understanding of the cards, so that when you're reading on a situation regarding a workplace conflict and Cups are coming up, you can resist the urge to conclude that the querent is experiencing a love affair at the office, unless there are very clear indicators to confirm that conclusion, or that their career issues are being caused by tensions in their love life.

A fantastic starting point is to consider the elements both present and absent in the spread and their interaction with the question. This will provide a great deal of information about the situation before you even interpret the cards. But, before we go any further, let's get into what I mean when I talk about elements.

What I present here is my own method. There are many other methods, other traditions, and other currents that may assign different elemental associations to the cards, especially to Court Cards, so feel free to use whatever option resonates the most with you as a reader.

The Elemental Correspondences of the Major Arcana

There are two different ways to work with elemental correspondences: a four-element method and a five-element method.

I used to assign the fifth element (Spirit, Ether, Akasha . . . whatever you want to call it) to Major Arcana cards and assign them a role of milestone or mission. To put it plainly, I assigned them a heightened significance. However, as I evolved in my journey, labeling the Major Arcana "extra mystical" by default stopped making sense to me, so I moved towards the elemental associations based on the astrological associations of the cards. Fear not! This is not going to turn into a complicated astrology book with a hundred correspondences. We will keep it simple and divide the cards into four groups.

Air Cards: The Fool, The Magician, The Lovers, Justice, The Star

Fire Cards: The Emperor, Strength, The Wheel of Fortune, Temperance, The Tower, The Sun, Judgement

Water Cards: The High Priestess, The Chariot, The Hanged Man, Death, The Moon

Earth Cards: The Empress, The Hierophant, The Hermit, The Devil, The World

The Elemental Correspondences of the Minor Arcana

Traditionally, the suit of Swords is associated with the element of air, Wands with fire, Cups with water, Pentacles with earth. There are some traditions that switch the elemental correspondences of Swords and Wands, so it's possible that you might encounter Swords as fire and Wands as air in certain decks. On a personal level, I cannot wrap my head around that. Sticks burn, so Wands are fire. Swords cut the air more often than flesh, and they involve a great deal of concentration, skill, and education in order to wield them, so it only makes sense for the suit of Swords to be associated with air.

Here is how we'll be assigning the elements in this book:

Suit of Swords: Air

Suit of Wands: Fire

Suit of Cups: Water

Suit of Pentacles: Earth

The Elemental Correspondences of the Court Cards

This is the part of the deck that causes the most debate when it comes to assigning an elemental correspondence. Things can get a bit trickier, because each rank of the court is assigned to an element, but simultaneously they also belong to the element of their suit. My explanation compares the courts to different representations of each element and makes it easier for the reader to integrate it.

Everyone seems to agree that Cups are undeniably water and Pentacles are undeniably earth. Most of the debate happens around Knights and Kings, and the elements of fire and air. It's fun to see how the active elements, fire and air, can inflame an inferno of disagreement when blended together!

You are likely to see people label Knights as air and Kings as fire. This does not make sense to me, personally. The historical figure of the knight is a doer, a fighter, a defender. Knights were the ones who would go into battle in the name of the king. The king, meanwhile, rules over his entire dominion, making decisions (for better or worse) for the supposed benefit of his people. You need way more air than fire to do that.

Pages correspond with the element of earth. They are the foundation of the suit, the starting point. They are similar to Aces in the sense that they possess the qualities of the element they represent but, by themselves, they lack direction.

Looking at it this way, the Page of Swords is Earth of Air. I like to think of them as the movement of the leaves or grass when a breeze blows. It can be gentle and refreshing, but too much air could also tear the leaf from the tree. The Page of Swords is not very well grounded and represents the most unstable of the pages.

The Page of Wands is Earth of Fire. The way I see them is as a spark that has the potential to catch and become a bigger fire. They have no control in determining what they will become, or whether the spark will catch at all. This page is definitely driven, but they are more equipped with motivation than with know-how.

The Page of Cups is Earth of Water. I see them as a sprout. A seed has been planted and watered, and it has now germinated. It's a promising start, even if there are no guarantees that it will grow into a solid tree yet. This page is in the early stages of promising growth, but it's important to note that they are still in a vulnerable stage.

The Page of Pentacles is Earth of Earth, which makes them a seed that has been planted. When a seed is planted, it is full of the potential of new life. It's hidden, so you can't see what is going on underneath. It needs time to sprout, and that process cannot be rushed. This is the slowest page, but also one of immense potential.

Knights correspond with the element of fire, although you may see them in correspondence with the element air in other material, especially if you follow the Golden Dawn tradition. They are doers and, based on their historical context, it doesn't make sense to me to associate them with air. I associate them with fire instead. They represent movement and their career has an expiration date, which often makes them temporary, like a quick blazing fire.

The Knight of Swords is Fire of Air. He is the take-no-prisoners kind of knight. Out of the four, he's the one that, in the traditional Rider Waite Smith depiction, seems to be riding at full speed, ready to attack. I think of him as a tornado. A tornado happens when hot, moist air meets cold, dry air, making it an accurate representation of the interaction of these two elements. Often unpredictable, this knight won't stop for anyone and has the potential to cause damage even if it is not his inherent intention. This is probably the fastest knight, if a bit of a zealous one.

The Knight of Wands is Fire of Fire. He is the go-getter. His original depiction shows a knight that's ready to ride and fulfill his mission. He can be hot-headed, as well as passionate about his cause. This is a pretty fast-acting knight who can get as hot as iron. He will definitely leave a mark in the right circumstances.

The Knight of Cups is Fire of Water. I think of him as boiling water. He is intense and heats up fast, but what happens to boiling water is that it eventually evaporates and leaves nothing behind. This is a knight that comes across as dedicated, but he's volatile in his commitment to the situation that's being asked about.

The Knight of Pentacles is Fire of Earth. He is the slowest knight. In his classical Rider Waite Smith depiction, he is the only one whose horse has all four legs on the ground. He's ready to go, but he first wants to know where he is going and how he is going to get there. He's the planner knight. I compare him to a bonfire, in the sense that he is grounded, and he is also within the boundaries defined by the task that he will complete. He won't rush into anything until there's some certainty about what happens next.

The Queens correspond with the element of water. They are passive when exercising their power. In their historical context, they were nurturers of the kingdom, and they secured their position when they secured the king's lineage. (Unfair, I know!)

The Queen of Swords is Water of Air. I think of her as the deep waters of the ocean. She's probably the least motherly queen, even though, as the ocean itself, she can still be home to those who find comfort in her characteristics. Just like a cold plunge, she is clear, sharp, straight to the point, and courageous.

The Queen of Wands is Water of Fire. In a way, I see her as a different aspect of boiling water. I would say she's probably hot oil. She's what you need to get that food cooked, but she's not going to go grocery shopping for you. Her nourishing side may be a bit tough love, but she is definitely goal and action oriented, and will give the best direction.

The Queen of Cups is Water of Water. I think of her as the water of the womb. She's nourishing like no other, provides a safe space, doesn't rush, and nourishes passively. She is there, consistently, but she is not necessarily interfering.

The Queen of Pentacles is Water of Earth. She is also nourishing, but in a different way. I think of her as a fruit tree. She is a provider and uses what she has created to nourish others. She will probably teach you how to care for your own garden. Her nourishing style is based on a generous spirit.

Kings are connected to the element of air. As previously mentioned, you may also see them as the element of fire in certain traditions. From my perspective, it doesn't make sense to me to portray the Kings as fire when they must exert control over the kingdom. The role of the king is diplomatic, and, while he is action oriented, it makes the most sense to me to think of them as air.

The King of Swords is Air of Air. I think of him as a flying eagle. He has a full view of what is going on, which allows him to make decisions based on facts. Not everyone may agree with these facts or understand them, but they have solid reasoning behind them.

The King of Wands is Air of Fire. I think of him as a cannon. He's powered by fire, by that heat, but he is also focused and has a clear mission that he is ready to fulfill. His drive and his passion are what keep him moving, but he does it with a clear objective in mind.

The King of Cups is Air of Water. I like to compare him with a skilled sailor who is familiar with his element. He knows when it's safe to navigate, as well as how and when to react when the seas get rough, but also when it would be better to stay away from those waters. He is in touch with his emotions, but not dominated by them. Air confers him the ability to navigate circumstances.

The King of Pentacles is Air of Earth. He's like a fortress on a mountain. Similarly to the King of Swords, his high view allows him insight into the circumstances that surround him, but he's not going to change his position. Rather, he will plan and adapt his moves based on the strategic fortress that he has built around himself. Safety is paramount for this king.

There's a commonly accepted traditional order for the suits in tarot: Wands, Cups, Swords and Pentacles, not that it matters much, but if you're familiar with that, you may have noticed by now that I follow a nontraditional order. This is because of the association of the suits with the elements. Air, Fire, Water, and Earth, or Swords, Wands, Cups, and Pentacles.

The rationale behind my method is that everything starts with an idea. Nothing comes to fruition without having been a seed in someone's mind. Air is the origin, even if it is intangible. That idea needs action, or fire, to travel from the world of ideas into the physical realm. It needs the vocation, the emotional investment of water and its nourishment, to ultimately turn into what we can see and feel, into something tangible, which is earth.

With that in mind, we can delve deeper into what the elements stand for and investigate what we can do with this information. This is key information for reading in any context.

Air: Usually associated with logical thinking and communication, air is so much more. Our mind is where we experience consciousness. Our brain doesn't make a distinction between thoughts and reality, so air is not always logical. It *can* be logical, but it can also be tumultuous and conflicting. It can be clarity, but it can also be confusion or self-deceit. It can be conflicting. It can be fear. It can be our greatest trap but also the source of liberation.

Air has a greater bearing than it's given credit for, and it has a whole spectrum of nuance to add to our interpretations.

Fire: Work and passion are two keywords that are often associated with this element, but of course there are many more. Fire is drive, survival, the most primal feelings. It can be anger, desire, or fuel. It can be one of the most powerful things that we experience: chemistry.

Fire is what makes us get up and put up a fight, what motivates us. It is what ignites within us, whether it makes sense or not, and pushes us beyond what we thought possible.

Water: This is the element of feelings and emotions. There is an undeniable association between water and romantic love, but romance is not the only option when it comes to associations. Water adds meaning. It is vocational, the love for what we do. It is spiritual, intuitive, and adaptable.

Water is changeable, transforming and cleansing. It can wash away excess and restore us to a natural, bare state.

Earth: This element is often heavily associated with financial matters, but it is also everything that is tangible. It is security, grounding, our foundation. Earth is what we can perceive through our senses, where we come from, and what we are going to leave behind when we are gone. This element has to do with our inheritance and with our legacy, and with what we build to last.

Earth is our home, our means, and our tangible resources—sometimes, even, our backup, what we have that can sustain us in a time of need.

With this outlook, we can begin to see how every situation can contain aspects of all four elements.

In the context of a romantic relationship, for example, air could refer to communication and plans, but it is also the domain in which idealization lives. Fire stands for the chemistry and passion between the couple. Water brings in love, nourishment, emotional connection. Earth brings stability and long-term potential to the mix.

While the presence all four elements would be desirable in this (and most) context, the ones that actually appear in the spread will tell us a lot about that relationship. If you pull a spread about romance and it's all Wands and Swords, or fire and air, you know that this can be a relationship full of conflict, one that lacks stability and emotional connection. It may be fueled by strong chemistry, but it has a component of uncertainty and wandering, as air suggests. With water and earth off the table, the relationship is missing the components that make it viable for the long term.

Let's think about this in the context of a career. Air refers to expression, the intellectual challenge, the know-how, the flow of ideas. Fire has to do with the workload and motivation, and also with potential conflict. Water deals with the vocational aspect, how meaningful the job is for the person, and also with creative and social aspects. Earth has to do with the financials, but also with the stability and long-term prospects for the querent.

An ideal job would probably have all the elements present, but, like the previous context we analyzed, there are some that could be more desirable or more significant than others. A person who values stability at the workplace may be happy to do without any water in the spread as long as the bills are paid. An individual with a highly vocational drive may be willing to sacrifice other aspects.

If we explore this from a financial perspective, air represents our budgeting and our financial plan, but also our worries about money. Fire can refer to what we do with the money, such as how it's spent and how far it can take us. Water can refer to the emotional aspect of spending or saving, our relationship with finances. Earth has to do with security, savings, property, inheritance, and legacy. It's the long-term financial plan.

In a spiritual context, we can see air as our spiritual connection and communication. It can also be the rational filter that we apply to spirituality. Fire relates to our practice. Water can be about the spiritual bond that we maintain with the entities of our choice, as well as our intuition, our faith. Earth represents how this spiritual practice affects our material life.

In matters pertaining to health, air can refer to the state of our mind or highlight our concerns. Fire is our mobility, our capacity to do things, our levels of energy and stamina. It's the systems that keep everything functioning. Water has to do with anything related to fluids: blood, lymph, acids, enzymes, semen, urine, and so on. It is also our emotional well-being. Earth has to do with our senses and what we perceive through them, our skin, and the state of our physical health.

If you follow this line of thought, you can find a way to assign the four elements to any context. The elements that are present on the table become as important as what's missing, or what is there but not showing its brightest side. (The Hanged Man is water, but it may not be the water that you would ideally want to have.) This gives you insight into the major energies or the current state of the matter, what has room for improvement, what is simply not there, and even what may be there in excess.

Elemental interactions are important too. A little bit of fire can be put out by air, like blowing out a birthday candle. If we have only a little drive to get something done, we can become paralyzed by our own planning and not follow through, putting out that fire. The right amount of air, though, can feed a small fire, but it can also inflame the fire to a point that it becomes destructive.

The interaction of water and fire is similar. Water can put out a fire. Fire can warm up water, but it also can make it boil and evaporate. It's all about the amount!

Earth and water are, a priori, two very compatible elements that can nurture a situation, but in the wrong circumstances they can also create mud, a puddle, or an overwatered plant that rots and dies.

Water and air stay in their own lanes in favorable circumstances, but in less ideal situations they are the ingredients of a mighty storm that can become destructive.

Air and earth similarly tend to mind their own business and not mingle. They need an additional element for something to grow—for instance, the drive of fire. However, they can turn into a sandstorm, bringing confusion and creating a mess.

Fire and earth can work together in the right context. Sometimes we need a controlled fire. However, if unattended, that fire can grow out of control, creating an undesirable circumstance. In the opposite direction, a large amount of dirt can put out a small fire, meaning too much stubbornness and planning can kill the drive to accomplish a goal.

Keeping in mind the interaction of the elements both within the context of the question and between themselves provides us with a rich frame to start our reading, even before getting into the specific card meanings. This is why it's one of the first steps that I take when interpreting a spread. These interactions will give you an idea of what is both available and unavailable to the querent, as well as any potential trouble, and even some hints as to actions that can be taken to redirect things to a desirable outcome.

Let's apply all of this in a sample three-card reading. Here is our question: "How will Morgan and Albert's first date go?"

If we explore the elements, we see earth with the Nine of Pentacles, fire with Strength, and air with the Six of Swords. Water is desirable in the context of a date, so its absence is noteworthy.

The earth in the Nine of Pentacles establishes a comfortable baseline for the date, while the fire in Strength suggests a degree of chemistry or advancement, but air does not bring a particularly positive aspect. In this case, with air as the outcome of a first date, we can conclude that it's unlikely there will be a second date.

Directionally speaking, when looking at the interactions between the elements, we can see that the figures in the Nine of Pentacles and Strength are facing each other, which suggests a positive interaction between these two elements, with earth allowing the fire to burn within certain parameters. However, Strength and the Six of Swords are back-to-back, suggesting a not-so-positive interaction between the two elements, with air walking away from the fire, indicating that the oxygen will run out and the fire will be put out. This is an example of the information you can get from the elemental interactions between the cards before you even get to the individual card meanings.

EXERCISE: Here's an exercise to help you see how the elemental disposition can offer information in different contexts. Use the Nine of Pentacles, Strength, and Six of Swords as the answer to the following questions. Consider the different nuances and context, and base your interpretation on the elements. Remember to examine what is present as well as what is absent and how it affects the question.

- Morgan and Albert are married. The question is, "What can help them regain the spark in their relationship?"
- "How will Sandra's new business do in its first quarter?"
- "Is it advisable for Terry to consider bringing an investor into his endeavor?"
- "Is the friendship between Beatrice and Helena worth their investment? "

Chapter 3

The Numbers

Numbers give us a pattern that adds information to our reading. While you can of course dive deep into numerology, here we're going to keep it simple. In my practice, I don't go deep into individual numbers, but I do pay attention to any patterns of numbers that appear in groups or that are repeated throughout the spread. The main things we are going to pay attention to when looking at numbers are the following.

Ascending numbers: This is a pattern where the spread starts with a lower number and climbs to a higher number. For instance, a three-card spread in which you have the Three of Swords, the Five of Cups, and the Ten of Wands. We can see that, in this case, a negative situation seems to go *in crescendo*. First, it starts with a betrayal, then the grieving of that betrayal, and then the aftermath of having to carry on despite it, depending on the interpretation the cards grant. This kind of pattern escalates a situation for better or worse in either positive or negative situations.

Descending numbers: Similarly, a pattern of descending numbers is when there is a tendency in the spread to travel from a higher number to a lower one. In the same example of a three-card spread, imagine that we start with the Nine of Swords, followed by the Four of Swords, and then the Two of Wands. We start with a concern, a fear or worry, and then we find some solace in the Four of Swords, which allows us to recollect our thoughts and enter the space of the Two of Wands, which brings awareness of our situation and what we have achieved.

Groups of numbers: We can identify this pattern in a spread when we have a majority grouping of low, middle, or high numbers.

I consider low number cards to be Ace to Three. A pattern of a group of low numbers speaks of a situation that is in its early stages and hasn't yet developed in full. We are setting the foundation, but nothing is settled yet. The situation can be a bit volatile, depending on what else is present on the table.

Middle numbers go from Four to Seven. A pattern of middle numbers suggests the meat of the situation. It might indicate a conflicting situation (let's not forget that the troublesome fives belong in this category), and it can speak to things that have yet to be resolved. This pattern usually tells us where the open fronts are, as well as their meaning.

High numbers go from Eight to Ten. They speak of a situation that is reaching a conclusion, whether satisfactory or not. This may tell us that a problem is close to reaching a resolution, or that the next stage of the matter at hand is close.

Repetition: Repetition is when we have multiple cards of the same number. For instance, we have three Aces in the spread, or we have four Fours, or we have two Sevens and two Tens, or two Fives and The Hierophant (the fifth card of the Major Arcana), just to name a few examples.

Again, this is when we need to take absence into consideration. If, as in the example above, there is a reading with the Ace of Swords, the Ace of Wands, and the Ace of Cups, it suggests an abundance of those energies but a lack of grounding, since the Ace of Pentacles is not present. This indicates that, while the matter is full of possibilities, there is also a weak area that needs attention.

The presence of four Fours could indicate a well-established situation with a solid foundation, but also one that is difficult to change and not as satisfactory as it could be. In the example of two Sevens and two Tens, the relationship between presence and absence can be observed, but also the relationship between the repeating cards in order to draw conclusions.

When the repetition is reinforced by a Major Arcana card, as in the case with two Fives and The Hierophant, we can observe the contrast between the two types of cards. The two Fives in the Minor Arcana speak of conflict, while The Hierophant brings stability. Depending on the rest of the cards on the table, one could conclude that conflict is deeply established in the dynamics of the situation and is difficult to remove.

While the cases below are not intrinsically a numeric pattern, I have decided to incorporate them into this lesson.

Doubling numbers: This refers to situations in which you have cards on the table that double the number of the same suit. This is not necessarily one after the other (though that makes for a very interesting occurrence) but rather in ascending order in reference to the timeline of the spread. For instance, the Three of Pentacles and the Six of Pentacles, or the Five of Cups and the Ten of Cups.

It's worth observing how, in the case of the Three of Pentacles, that collaboration between cards can lead to sharing the resources obtained with the Six of Pentacles. When ill-aspected, on the other hand, it can also show a collaboration that brings a sense of entitlement when determining who is deserving of what, with one of the participants feeling like they're the judge of it.

In the case of the Five of Cups and the Ten of Cups, an apparent loss may actually lead to a satisfactory outcome when it is positively aspected, or to the closure of a cycle that is brought to completion under a less favorable light.

Halving numbers: This is the contrary case in which the cards are halved in the order in which they appear in the spread. For example, if we have the Ten of Pentacles and the Five of Pentacles, this would be an indicator of diminishing resources throughout the development of the situation, or that there will be a loss of stability or material security, or an outright financial loss.

An alternative example would be the Two of Wands and the Ace of Wands, in which a planning stage could revert back to being just an idea or an urge without the means to materialize just yet.

Even and odd numbers: A pattern of even numbers can be an indication that the situation is balanced or, at the very least, stable, while a pattern of odd numbers can be a sign of a more chaotic situation. If you think of a spread with the Two, Four, and Six of Wands, it would appear that things are under control. On the other hand, a spread with the Five of Pentacles, Three of Swords, Five of Wands, and Seven of Cups leaves things a bit more up in the air.

Basics of Numerology

Here is a quick crash course on the meanings behind the numbers of each card.

One (Ace): One is the origin of all, the potential, power. The Aces in tarot relate to the raw potential of the number one, as does The Magician, the card that represents the number one in the Major Arcana. (The Fool, the first card, represents number zero.) The Magician possesses the ability to transform the elements into anything that they need to be. A significant presence of number One cards in a reading highlights the power of potential in the situation.

Two: Duality, partnership, balance, intuition, decision. Twos highlight the importance of looking beyond the self and instead contemplating what else is needed to make things work. That could be a partnership, or the need to balance two priorities, or two different areas of life. It brings forth the connection between our inner and outer perception, fostering the growth of our intuition, which connects us with The High Priestess. A significant amount of number Two cards in a reading makes us ponder what or whom we need to connect to, highlights the other piece of the puzzle, or highlights the need to choose a path.

Three: Expansion, communication, growth. Threes are expansive. This number incorporates things, whether that's people, new knowledge, new energy. It's about fostering growth and aiming higher, a meaning connected with the nurturing and growing energy of The Empress. A significant amount of Threes in the reading can point towards a tendency for growth (even though it can sometimes be painful) and a need to reach out to others.

Four: Stability, foundation, pragmatism. Four is the number of structure and order, and acts as a pillar upon which to build. It has a certain rigidity within itself that bodes well with The Emperor and calls for authority over the situation. A significant amount of Fours in the reading suggest that things are well established, which can be a positive addition to the reading. However, in certain contexts, it speaks of a situation so fixed that it is difficult to change or move without being very intentional about it.

Five: Challenge, dynamism, exploration. In tarot, Fives are not easy, especially in the Minor Arcana, so an abundance of number Fives present in your readings highlights the need to change direction, as the original plan isn't likely to bear fruit. The Hierophant seems to be in opposition to this call for dynamism, however, being the earthly representative of the divine. The Hierophant brings a transformation of sorts numerologically, acting as a channel between the human and the divine.

Six: Harmony, cooperation, healing, union. Six is a positive number that brings a sense of balance to a situation and generally points towards an improvement. It's a number connected to the emotional aspect and to relationships, and what makes The Lovers relevant numerologically. A significant number of Sixes in a reading speaks of a harmonious environment, highlights the importance of connections, and brings a feeling of progress and healing.

Seven: Reflection, wisdom, perception. Sevens are a "think before you act" kind of number. A significant number of Sevens in a reading highlights the importance of knowledge and strategy, and suggests that consideration is required before action is taken. This card connects with the essence of The Chariot and the Socratic myth of the charioteer, which, long story short, describes the charioteer as the intellectual force tasked with driving the chariot with two horses: one that represents our higher calling and a second one that represents our lower impulses.

Eight: Endurance, dedication, ambition. Eight is a strong number that signifies perseverance, consistency, and mastery. This number, connected with the Strength card, doubles down on the stability of four to bring things to the next level. A significant number of Eights in a reading highlights the need to refocus, persist, and rearrange priorities to continue in the pursuit of our goals.

Nine: Awareness, support, transition, transformation. Nine is a very spiritual number that relates to transitional processes. It is also close to endings. Related to The Hermit, number nine deals with inner wisdom. A significant number of Nines in a reading can indicate that there is too much noise or too many open fronts that are about to undergo a transformation. It encourages the querent to look within for answers and guidance on how to proceed.

Ten: In the context of tarot, ten is the number of completion. Ironically, it is connected with The Wheel of Fortune, which represents a cycle again. An abundance of Tens in the reading indicates that the current chapter of the querent's life, or at least of the situation that they are inquiring about, is coming to an end and that what comes next is about to be revealed.

Pro tip: If you have multiple cards of the same number in a reading, pay attention to what suits are missing to enrich your interpretation.

Look at this sample reading and pay attention to the numerological aspect. The spread above is a Nine Card Tableau, which we'll learn about later.

The question is: "Is it the right moment to move in with my partner?"

How many of the above patterns do you perceive in the tableau?

Focusing on the numerological aspect, there are three things that stand out. First, there are three Fours (Four of Pentacles, The Emperor, Four of Swords) and two Twos (Two of Pentacles, Two of Wands). There is doubling from the Ace of Pentacles to the Two of Pentacles, and halving from the Four of Pentacles to the Two of Pentacles. There are low and middle numbers but no high numbers.

This suggests a promising beginning and a situation with momentum, but an excessive focus on certainty and security with the Fours can cause a loss of traction. Starting out with an Ace as the nuance card (that's the card on the top left corner, but don't worry about it for now) is almost invariably a good thing, and the Ace of Pentacles speaks of a solid opportunity. The Four of Pentacles and The Emperor couldn't be more positively aspected, which reinforces that there is an existing foundation that warrants taking this next step.

With that said, there is such a thing as too much of a good thing. When the initial potential of the Ace of Pentacles is turned into the doubt of the Two of Pentacles, the Four of Swords decelerates the progress, and the conservativism of the Two of Wands leaves things stagnated.

This is a basic interpretation, rooted for the most part in the numerological aspect, without getting deeper into specific card meanings. However, you can always come back to this spread to make a more elaborate interpretation with all the elements of the Nine Card Tableau.

If we return to the question, "Is this the right moment to move in with my partner?" then the answer would be yes. It is the right moment, but there is a limited window of opportunity before overthinking delays the decision.

To sum it up, the numerological aspects of the cards can give us hints of the overall energy of the situation and how that energy is used or distributed. In those instances where there is significant repetition, it may also point to a general theme in the reading.

Chapter 4

Color and Body Language

How each reader views the symbolism of the cards is unique, based on their own experiences and understanding of the world. Where one reader may see a mountain in the spread as representing an obstacle, another may see it as a sacred pilgrimage. Even with symbols whose meanings are somewhat universally agreed upon, there will be schools of thought that delve deeper than others. In this chapter, we explore some general but relevant symbolism, focusing mainly on the background colors of the cards and on the body language of the figures.

This chapter's exploration is strongly based on the classic Rider Waite Smith deck, but there's nothing to stop you from applying these insights to the deck of your choice. Separate the cards in your deck based on either their background or predominant colors. Do you see any patterns? You will probably discover that there is a commonality that helps you identify those groups of cards that may contain an additional message.

In the classic Rider Waite Smith, we find just a handful of predominant colors in the backgrounds: different hues of blue, yellow, gray, and black. Paying attention to the overall tone of the colors of the reading can give us insight into the climate of the situation we are reading on.

Generally, cards with blue backgrounds tend to add openness or at least neutrality to the reading. This color doesn't present a challenge by itself, and finding a group of cards with blue backgrounds may speak of a period of clearer skies.

The cards with yellow backgrounds are usually promising, active, and strong. They bring potential into the reading and open a window of opportunity and success.

Cards with predominantly gray backgrounds tend to add a nuance of stillness or stagnation. They may represent a situation that is dull, inactive, or one that doesn't offer a lot of wiggle room to bring change.

Those cards with black backgrounds are among the most challenging in the deck. A cluster of black and gray cards can be an indicator that we're dealing with a closed avenue, or that the conditions are not favorable.

Delving Deeper into Color

What about colors that, for some reason, seem to "pop out" to you during a reading? Have you ever seemed to notice a new element of color even though you have seen that card three thousand times before? Noticing seemingly smaller red elements as a significant pattern in the reading can be an indicator that the situation is full of intensity or passion, or is somewhat "raw," or that there is a visceral component to it. Sometimes, it's the white elements that seem more noticeable, which suggests that the querent may be coming into the situation with an innocent heart, but also that they are protecting themselves, or that they are trying to get to the bottom of the situation.

The meaning of colors can vary widely depending on region, cultural context, and even individual situation. While white is often considered a color of purity in the West, in some Eastern regions it is a color of mourning, and in certain magical practices or religions, it can be a color of protection. My advice to you is to find whatever meaning makes the most sense to you for each color and apply it to your readings as an additional layer. This does not have to be done in an exhaustive way, but rather in a way that adds richness and substantiation to your interpretations.

Body Language

The majority of decks, whether they feature human figures or animal ones, contain some degree of body language. You can use this body language to identify patterns in in your reading. While we are focusing on the Rider Waite Smith, you can easily use these practices to decipher the body language in your favorite deck. Insert the cards mentioned in groups as you see fit.

SITTING:

If we look at the cards in the image, we can see that all the figures that appear are sitting, but there are differences. What do the Nine of Cups, The Sun, the Eight of Pentacles, and the Four of Cups have in common? Despite the differences in their meaning, the body language of all four figures suggests a comfortable position, even though the comfort of the Nine of Cups may not be the same comfort as the Eight of Pentacles. When looking at The Emperor and Justice, we can see that their position is somewhat forceful. It's a position of authority, but they seem to own it. It is not a natural position, but rather one constricted by their role. In the case of the Two of Swords and the Four of

Pentacles, we can see that, while they are sitting, they are definitely not comfortable. They are sitting because it is necessary to maintain their position, but their inaction is forced by the circumstances. If they were to move, they would not be able to continue with their task.

STANDING:

If we now look at the second image, we see that all the figures are standing, but their body language is not the same. The Fool, The Magician, and the Three of Wands present body language that speaks to openness. They appear comfortable in their situation, but they are also ready to do something else. The Two of Pentacles is dynamic, but focused. He cannot abandon the task at hand. His movement is cyclic. Something similar happens with the Nine of Wands. While his movement is more static than dynamic, he is in a position that cannot be abandoned, and his body language is protective as well as tired.

Both the Five of Cups and the Seven of Pentacles are slouching, contemplating a situation that cannot be helped. The fruits will not grow faster if the person in the Seven of Pentacles keeps watch, and the spilled wine will not return to the cups no matter how much the cloaked figure keeps staring at them. The body language in both cases is somewhat defeated. It is not indicative of movement, nor is it productive.

We can examine something similar with open body posture (open arms, open chest, separated legs) and closed body posture (guarded chest, crossed arms, crossed or close legs). This kind of body language offers information about the state of the querent, of the situation, or of a person relevant to the reading.

Let's practice with an example. This time, we will make our interpretation based on the body language of figures in the cards.

Sarah had a strong argument with her brother a few weeks ago and they are currently not on speaking terms. She would like to know if the relationship between them can be repaired.

Interestingly, the two figures that appear in The Tower are in freefall, having lost control. Their arms and legs are spread, and they have intense expressions on their faces. This is a good representation of the falling out that Sarah and her brother experienced. Next, we have The Empress, with a calm and collected semblance. The Six of Pentacles is the next card, where a figure with a fairly open posture is tending to two others whose body language is more closed. However, their palms are up, willing to receive.

An interesting thing to note here is that the first card shows two people, the second card shows one person, and the third card shows three individuals.

The transition from the aggressive/panicked posture in the first card, to the collected posture of the second one, to the three figures in the last card tells a story. The relationship will be restored, but a mediator will need to help each party see their own contribution to the current situation.

Again, this is taking into consideration only one single layer of interpretation, without getting into the meanings of the cards. I invite you to practice this method of interpretation. It can be challenging at first to separate the card meanings from their body language. I suggest that, as an exercise, you ask a question, whether real or hypothetical, and try to answer it with a three-card pull where you base your interpretation solely on the body language of the cards.

Extra exercise: Try combining the interpretative techniques we have learned so far and apply them to this spread. See what that adds to your interpretation.

Chapter 5

Aspects or Reversals?

Now that we have known each other for a few chapters, it's time for me to make a confession . . . I don't read reversals! At least, not in the traditional sense. If you're not familiar with reversals, here's a brief explanation. Using reversals is the deliberate inclusion of upside-down cards in the reading, often altering their meaning in a variety of ways: the opposite of its upright meaning, an unavailable energy, or a blockage, to name a few.

I do not physically reverse the cards. I find it distracting and unnecessary when following the tableau method. If you wish to incorporate reversals into your tableau readings, you are of course free to do so, but it will mess up things like directionality and interactions.

Because the tableau method is based on the interactions between cards, threading the interpretation of the reading through the spread as a whole, introducing reversals seems redundant. I do have students who have chosen to incorporate reversals into their readings, so while I recommend coming in with an open mind if you are a reader who incorporates reversals, it is ultimately up to you whether you keep them in your readings.

In the tableau method, the individual card is not as relevant as its context in the larger picture. It is supported by every other factor that plays a part in the reading, such as color, numerology, or body language, but mostly its interaction with neighboring cards and the question. In tableau, instead of having an upright and reversed meaning, the cards are seen as a whole, with their lights and shadows. The cards around them will reveal the aspect, positive or negative, that is shining at that particular moment. In that sense, each card is like a person. We all show different aspects of ourselves depending on context. We don't behave the same at work as at home. We don't behave the same with a neighbor as we do with a friend or a lover. Sometimes we must be polite, and sometimes we are angry and lose our temper. The cards act in a similar way. With observation and practice, you will learn to differentiate the aspect that the card is showing.

Let me give you an example using a card that has a reputation as universally good, with virtually no downside at all: The Sun.

I won't say that The Sun is not a card of merriment, joy, and positive outcomes, because it is. If we were to view The Sun in a little bit of a neutral light, it can indicate "getting our way." However, getting what we want is not always a good thing. The surrounding cards will determine if we are tilting towards a truly positive outcome, or if the meaning leans more towards momentary satisfaction, only to discover later that, after all, everything is not all that shiny.

Speaking of shiny, The Sun can also be blinding. It can keep us from seeing other options when we are solely focused on achieving this one thing that we perceive as the be-all and end-all. Too much light can sometimes get in the way of seeing clearly.

Here is an opposite example using the Ten of Swords. This is a card that nobody likes to see in a reading. It speaks of defeat, backstabbing, abandonment, neglect, and an assortment of miseries. But it can also tell us that this is as bad as the situation is going to get, and the only direction to go from here is up. It can be a freeing card, one that puts an end to a series of calamities and opens the door to things to come when viewed in the right context.

So, how do we know which aspect of a card to interpret?

The first step I take when I look at the cards is to see if they seem to favor the subject, question, or situation, or if they are presenting an obstacle or offer opposition. If we are pulling three cards for the question "Will Jack and Jessica move in together?" then we probably want to see cards of agreement, movement, and stability. A textbook positive answer could be the Two of Cups—The Chariot—the Four of Wands. This answer speaks of the commitment of moving in together, with the actual move represented by The Chariot and the Four of Wands.

Now, with that same question in mind, let's say that The Chariot is still in the mix, but instead of being in between the Two of Cups and the Four of Wands, the sequence is Nine of Swords—The Chariot—Five of Wands. While The Chariot by itself would be supportive of the idea of moving in together, the fact that it is between the Nine of Swords and the Five of Wands suggests that the couple will not move in together, at least not for now, as there are concerns and fears. This spread seems to be leading to a place of conflict between the couple, such as a disagreement or an inability to see eye-to-eye about the next steps. The Chariot in this particular context is much the same as if you were to physically use a reversal.

Another thing to take into consideration is whether the surrounding cards are supporting the original energy and meaning of an individual card. A Ten of Cups that is surrounded by supportive cards—for instance, something equally joyous such as The Sun, or a not-so-bright but still collaborative Three of Pentacles—will speak of blissful happiness, familial union, a long-term successful agreement, a developing vocation, or other desirable things. However, in a spread full of cards that oppose the question—for example, the Five of Cups or the Eight of Swords—the Ten of Cups outcome is more likely to say, "this is as good as it's going to get," than it is to say, "against all odds, this situation will turn around."

Pay attention to the interaction between the cards and the question, as well as among the cards themselves, to get a sense of whether they are positively or ill-aspected.

When in doubt, here are a couple of tricks to help you determine the aspect of the cards.

- Ask yourself "What makes the most sense in this situation?" This is a simple yet powerful way of determining how to interpret a card. You can even make two interpretations in your mind, one with the card positively aspected, one with the card negatively aspected, so you can see what feels like a natural addition to the rest of the reading.
- Don't let one card carry the entire weight of the reading. Sometimes we have a very lackluster spread, but The Sun is somewhere in the mix, so we jump to the conclusion that everything will be wonderful because The Sun is there, ignoring everything else. Or, on the contrary, we can have a pretty decent combination of cards with The Tower in the mix, and think that everything is going to hell in a handbasket. When you have a card that you are tempted to give that amount of weight to, consider a different aspect and you will very often see that it fits better.

Remember that you can also use the colors present in the card, the elemental aspects, the numerology, and the interactions between the cards themselves to help you with this.

Auspicious versus Inauspicious Placements

This is a cartomantic technique that is based on the position of the cards in regards to a significator card. A significator card is a specific card that represents a querent or someone who is significant in the reading. In tarot, the Court Cards are usually used as significators, though there are other options that we will explore. These significator cards don't always clearly present themselves, so here are two methods to determine their auspicious and inauspicious sides. Which method you use depends on the card and on the deck that you are using.

If you are using a Rider Waite Smith deck, some Court Cards face either the right or the left. For instance, the Queen of Swords faces the right and presents her back to the left, while the King of Wands faces the left and presents his back to the right.

In this scenario, the auspicious placement will be whatever lies in the direction they are looking, while the inauspicious placement will be whatever lies in the direction they have turned their backs on.

If we look at the King of Swords, we can see that he is facing forwards. His head is not tilted in a direction that favors one side over another. With cards that present facing forward, that have no clear directional favor, or if you are using a deck in which these directionalities don't apply, the easiest way to determine the aspect is to use the right side as the auspicious side and the left side as the inauspicious side.

What does this mean in a practical way? Let's see it play out with an example.

Consider the direction the King of Wands is looking. We can see that the Eight of Swords is on the auspicious side, and the Ten of Wands on the inauspicious side.

While this combination makes it seem like he's between a rock and a hard place, we can interpret that the way to handle the situation is favored by inaction until all factors are known. In other words: Wait and see. Doing nothing and waiting for the situation to develop before making a decision is favorable to him. What is inauspicious is taking on a significant load without a clear aim, for the effort would not be fruitful with the Ten of Wands in that position.

The opposite combination, in which the Ten of Wands is on the auspicious side and the Eight of Swords is on the inauspicious side, would give a slightly different message. In this case, persevering in his actions or decisions despite the difficulties favors him. This is despite the difficulties represented by the Eight of Swords on the inauspicious side, which suggests that he could feel guilty or trapped in the situation, or that there is relevant information that he has yet to be able to unveil.

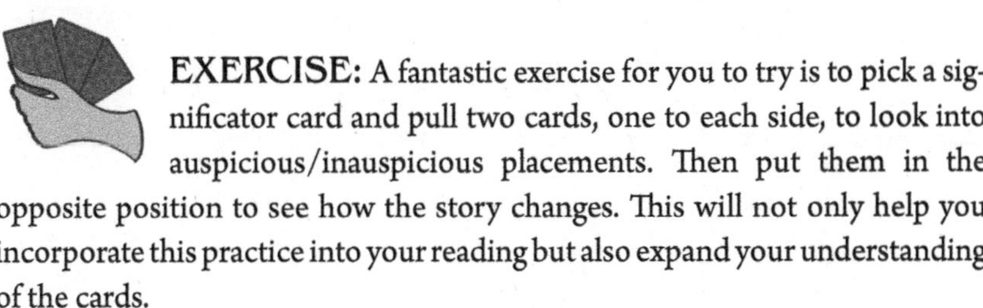

EXERCISE: A fantastic exercise for you to try is to pick a significator card and pull two cards, one to each side, to look into auspicious/inauspicious placements. Then put them in the opposite position to see how the story changes. This will not only help you incorporate this practice into your reading but also expand your understanding of the cards.

Chapter 6

Narrative Reading Technique

Understanding and dominating narrative reading is the foundation of the tableau system. As we approach the second part of the book, in which we will explore the flagship of the system, the Nine Card Tableau, it's important that this narrative reading technique is well understood before moving forward.

The narrative technique helps us move past classic positional reading, in which each card is bound to its own position, and increase our ability to turn the cards into a storyline, in which each arcana is connected to the next and together they weave a story. There is a loose structure that works pretty much like reading a Roman alphabet text: from left to right, from top to bottom. For now, we are going to be working with a single row of three or five cards.

To extract the most information from this technique, you can apply the other techniques that we have learned so far, such as the elemental interactions, or looking for patterns of color, numbers, and attitudes or body positions, as well as what's present and absent in the spread. You are not always going to have to go through each and every possible layer of interpretation, but it is always useful to think of them as tools that are at your disposal to help your overall interpretation.

Three-Card Narrative Reading Exercise

The best way to explain how this technique works is to go through a series of readings. We'll walk through the thought process of the narrative creation first, simply by putting together a story, and then we will apply it to different questions.

The picture on page 52 shows a three-card spread with The Wheel of Fortune, the Eight of Wands, and the Two of Pentacles.

From an elemental perspective, we have two fire cards (The Wheel of Fortune and the Eight of Wands) and one earth card (the Two of Pentacles). Air and water aren't present in the reading.

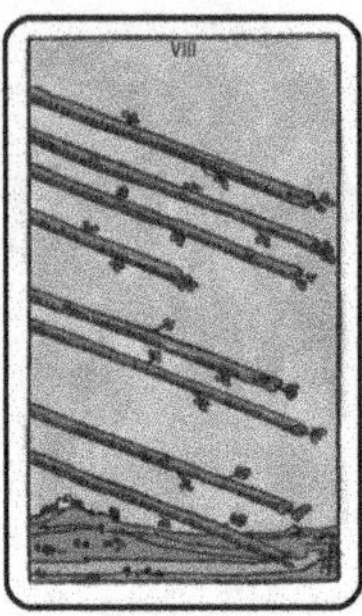

How do these cards affect one another? What do they have in common?

All of these cards have a nuance of movement to them, even a suggestion of speed. The Eight of Wands speeds up the Wheel of Fortune, and the Two of Pentacles keeps that motion going. The focused action of the Eight of Wands is necessary to keep the two pentacles in the air. Despite the presence of earth with the Two of Pentacles, it's a very dynamic card. The juggler needs to be well grounded in order to maintain their spinning disks. On the other hand, there's not a moment of rest.

This spread tells us a story about a somewhat hectic situation. This situation keeps moving. It doesn't quite settle, nor does it necessarily progress. The Two of Pentacles is a dance. The disk that's in one hand is now in the air. It changes to the other hand while the second disk is now up in the air. However, the cycle doesn't take us anywhere.

Now that we have our story, let's look at this spread from different perspectives, using this trio of cards to answer three different questions.

"Is it a good idea to keep my day job for a few more months while I grow my side business?"

These cards are pretty positive to that end, with a caveat. If the querent does not want to get stuck indefinitely juggling both their day job and their side business, it is necessary to bring the focus of the Eight of Wands to the table to establish their priority. This way there is a point in keeping them both going, as one of the options sustains the other. However, the querent must have a moment in mind in which the big wheel (the Wheel of Fortune) can roll on its own and gain full traction. Otherwise, it will get stuck in the same aimless motion. The earth present, while dynamic, needs a bit more focus to be grounded. The action of fire, while powerful, needs a bit of methodical thinking, since air is nowhere to be found in the reading, and the earth that is present is not very earthy. It would be beneficial to the querent's success to try and bring some more air into the equation with a solid plan, deadlines, and alternative contingencies.

"Will my ex and I get back together?"

Here the story can differ a little bit. The answer is probably yes, but that is not necessarily a good thing. This would be a textbook on-again, off-again relationship. The dominant force in the situation is fire but, with the aimlessness of the Two of Pentacles, there is no evolution to the relationship. It's possible that this couple can't be separated for an excessively long period of time, but they won't remain together for long after the reconciliation, either. The relationship is based in chemistry, with fire as a driving force, and sheer habit, which is the present earth, but it lacks a plan and the emotional connection to make it work, considering the absence of air and water.

"Will my partner propose?"

We are dealing with a no. The relationship will surely continue, but the dynamics in the cards suggest that there is an inertia to the relationship that is not going to change anytime soon. The querent's partner appears to be okay with the way things are between them and does not wish to create a change, but rather to continue things as they are. There may be "spur of the moment" discussions, but they are not followed through with planning or action. While the reading does not show the dissolution of the relationship, it also does not show any plans to change the current dynamic between them.

Now we are going to answer the same questions with a different trio of cards.

Having two out of three cards be Court Cards is probably a nightmare for the beginner reader, but this is a fantastic lesson in looking at the interpretation of these cards without them necessarily representing people.

Let's ask our questions again and see what story the new cards are telling.

"Is it a good idea to keep my job for a few more months while I grow my side business?"

The combination of elements in this one is quite promising, as is the order of the cards. First we have water, which can allude to the vocational aspect in one's career, the thing that we really want to do or that seed that has just sprouted. That combined with the double fire of the Knight can grow towards the stability of the earth brought by the Four of Pentacles. This is definitely an indicator of growth and suggests that it is a good and sustainable idea.

And yet, curiously enough, there is a warning present that is similar to the previous reading. Waiting too long or being too conservative in the approach can lead to undesirable results. It's wise to keep the job for a bit longer, but not so long that it becomes a liability. It's important to use one's resources wisely and to know when to let go in order to make the best decisions. The absence of air once again suggests that having a plan before deciding that the safety net is no longer necessary will help keep things moving.

"Will my ex and I get back together?"

In this case, we can see that there is a reminiscent interest with the Page of Cups, and that the Knight of Wands can bring an impromptu reconnection, but that, essentially, the status of the situation doesn't change with the Four of Pentacles. The Four of Pentacles tries to have its cake and eat it too, which is not a great omen for a relationship. There may be an ongoing connection between the querent and their ex, but if commitment issues existed prior to the relationship, or there were incompatibilities between their long-term plans, those things will not be resolved.

If there were a reconciliation, the Four of Pentacles signifies that there would not be a significant change in the relationship. I wouldn't entirely close the possibility of getting back together, but I would not expect the relationship to be any different. It will have the same issues, conflicts, and incompatibility that ended it the first time around. While the Four of Pentacles brings earth, that earth is "boxed" within the walls of the castle. It cannot change its shape. The Page and the Knight can make for a torrid comeback, but it's one where, when reality settles in, so will dissatisfaction.

"Will my partner propose?"

This combination suggests a reluctant yes. A "shut-up ring," if you will. There isn't a plan to propose, as indicated by the absence of air. The Page of Cups brings an emotional component to the equation, but not a sense of readiness. The Knight of Wands adds a sense of haste and impulsivity to the decision, but the Four of Pentacles seems to bring that action to a stalemate. There's movement, surely, but rather than following through, it's aimed at keeping the peace. The partner doesn't want to let go of the relationship, but they don't want to make any real change either. While I could see a "yes" to the question of a proposal, especially in a context in which there is some sort of ultimatum at play, it appears to me a reluctant one.

In all these instances, we can see how the progression from Page to Knight turns a seed into action, which is in itself a positive, but water and fire don't usually go far, and the Four of Pentacles doesn't aspect this combination in a particularly positive way. While the answer to all three questions can be a yes, it is a yes with a warning or a caveat to consider.

Now that we have seen a couple of examples with three-card spreads, let's move on to the five-card version. The mechanics are the same, but having five cards to work with instead of three will allow us to consider many more factors; the elemental interactions are richer in a five-card layout than in a three-card one; and there are greater chances for interesting number combinations, interactions, and, in general, more information.

Five-Card Narrative Reading Exercise

Look at these five cards and try to build a story with them.

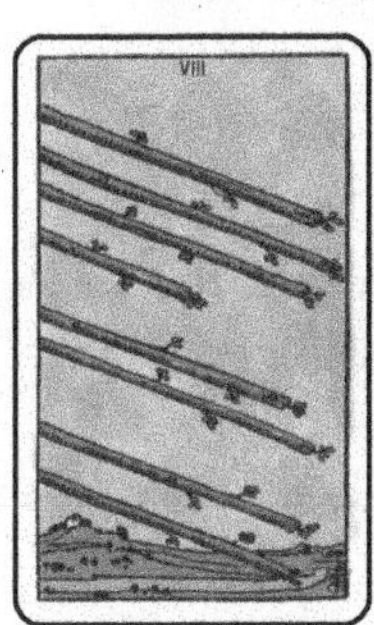

We have something interesting to consider: All four elements are present, all of the cards are minor arcana, and four out of five cards are even numbers.

As we saw previously, an even-number card majority in a spread tends to show a stable situation. The card furthest to the right, the outcome card, is an odd number, tilting that balance. We will see why in a moment.

There is also a double eight at beginning with the Eight of Wands and the Eight of Pentacles. There are two different ways to see this story, depending on the kind of context we want to give it. On the one hand, there is the possibility that the focus of the Eight of Wands in combination with the repetitive nature of the Eight of Pentacles leads to the movement and progress of the Six of Swords. Alternatively, the quick-paced nature of the Eight of Swords can clash with the masterful repetitiveness of the Eight of Pentacles and create a need to escape with the Six of Swords.

What defines this story, in my experience, is the Four of Swords appearing right after the Six. This card is disrupting the others, stopping all motion, and, in particular, halting the motion of the Six of Swords. This creates a need to contemplate before taking a step further and, with the Ace of Cups, find a path or a reason that moves the querent to commit to the next step.

The combination between the Eight of Wands, the Eight of Pentacles, and the Six of Swords suggests an inertia broken by a card that changes the flow of the reading. A new alternative appears with an Ace, the only odd number that appears in the reading.

This could be, for instance, the story of an individual who is studying a legacy career. Their great-grandfather was a doctor, their grandfather was a doctor, their father is a doctor, so of course this person is studying medicine. They probably have Roman numerals behind their name, and they are expected to add a few more letters to the queue! The problem, though, is that the querent's heart is not in it. There was never a question as to what they would do with their life, so their entire life was a race to repeat what the family had already mastered. Once caught in that inertia, they stop and realize that they need to find their own vocation.

It is precisely the element of water that shows up with an odd number. The Ace of Cups is full of potential and possibilities, breaking the pattern of even numbers that the cards have shown so far. Water is an element that had not made an appearance in the spread before and that is now showing up against the more practical elements, emerging as a new calling.

How would we interpret this row of five cards in the context, for instance, of a querent that would like to look into the development of an established romantic relationship that is in decline?

In that case, the inertia would also apply. The focus is on the routine, and the direction of the relationship is lost. This leads to a stagnation in which there is neither open conflict nor connection. This stalemate could lead to the need to take some sort of break from the relationship as they know it, as that Four of Swords disrupts the movement of the other cards. This break will allow them to reconnect with their motivation to be in the relationship, getting back in touch with the emotional aspect that was being taken for granted and unwillingly lost in the everyday routine.

What if the question is "Will my business be financially prosperous?"

While the reading is far from negative, I would like to see some more earth to substantiate financial prosperity in the reading. The Eight of Wands and Eight of Pentacles highlight the demanding nature of the business that will require the querent's input, attention, and resources in order to keep moving. But this is going to grow only so far with the Six of Swords being disrupted by the Four of Swords.

This suggests that the business's growth could reach a plateau where it would be difficult to move past a certain point. The Ace of Cups, though, adds a meaning to the endeavor that goes beyond the practicalities, suggesting that it may remain a passion project or something that the querent keeps on the side, for nothing in the reading suggests that it is going to end. Nothing suggests that it will make enough money for it to be considered prosperous, either.

This is an example of what I call finding substantiation in the reading. It requires the reader to really stick to the question, in this case the question of prosperity, and see if the cards are confirming or negating that desired outcome. In this case, there is nothing that confirms that prosperity, but there is also nothing that declares the project has completely failed. When there is no substantiation that things will go in a definitive way, it is time to investigate the gray areas.

In this example, we have a pretty positive outcome card. It's just not one that indicates material prosperity. Rather, it's one that speaks about vocational fulfillment, finding meaning in what one chooses to do, or in deciding that this project brings enough joy to continue while accepting that there can be certain limitations to the financial abundance that it is able to create.

This is one of the cases in which I would suggest continuing the reading with other questions, such as, "What changes would make this business more likely to become financially prosperous?" or "What would be a good way to combine this project with another, more sustainable one?" This way we can try to find solutions that lead to the querent's desired outcome.

Checklist

Remembering to combine the reading with the techniques that we have learned so far can be a bit overwhelming at first. Going through this checklist will help you pay attention to our varied techniques until layered reading becomes second nature for you.

- Consider the elemental interactions in the spread and how they affect the nature of the question. Considering how different aspects of the context are represented by different elements can help you understand the factors at play, as well as those that are missing, and how they work together.

- Look at the flow of the reading. Are the cards in harmony? Is there a "bumpy" disposition? Is there something that clashes noticeably with the rest of the cards?

- Check the numbers. Is there a tendency for the cards to travel upwards or downwards? Any repeating numbers? Does the spread mostly consist of low, middle, or high numbers?

- Colors and body language: Is there a dominant color in the spread? If so, how does it affect the reading? Is there a pattern in the posture of the figures in the cards that indicates something about the question?

- Have you found enough evidence in your reading to substantiate a favorable answer to your question? Or an unfavorable one? If neither, you may need to expound on the original question and investigate the gray areas.

What you have learned so far may be a lot of information to take in, particularly if you are either new at reading tarot or used to reading card by card. It is natural if you feel overwhelmed at first! It takes a while to integrate all of these techniques into your reading repertoire, and it is not necessary to use all of them at the same time.

We have already gone through some of the basics in preparation for the next part of the book where we will begin to read in a tableau disposition. If you are not sure that you are equipped to continue with the following techniques, my advice is that you continue reading anyway—often, it "clicks" when you see it all at work—and that you do a second reading later.

Part II

TABLEAU READING

HAVING TRAVELED THROUGH the first part of the book, you are now equipped to take the next step into tableau reading. Before, we were warming up and making connections in order to facilitate the learning process. Now we're going to delve into the system that will revolutionize your readings.

At first, the learning curve for tableau reading might feel a bit steep. You might feel overwhelmed. Think of it like learning to drive, or cook, or learning a complicated dance. You may feel at first that the task requires more eyes, hands, and feet than you have, and your attention is divided. But over time and with practice, this will become second nature. You won't even have to think about it.

Remember: You don't need to go through every single interpretive layer and apply every single technique every single time. These are tools for you to utilize. Sometimes the answer to your question will be evident at first glance. At other times, your answer may not be as obvious initially, but after applying a couple of interpretive steps, you will be able to see what the cards are indicating. Other times, you may have to dig deeper for the answer.

It is my belief that the cards answer the question asked. Virtually any question can be answered with tarot. When you stop trying to forcibly see something that isn't there, you'll discover that reading is easier than you may think.

In this part of the book, I will walk you through the Nine Card Tableau, the flagship of the system and the most versatile spread that you will ever see. Later, we will look through the 5x5 Tableau, a twenty-five-card spread that follows the same system, only expanded. The 5x5 Tableau will add everything that you need to know on the rare occasion you feel that the Nine Card Tableau isn't enough, or in those moments in which you are dealing with a more substantive timeline. Last but definitely not least, we'll learn about the Major Arcana Tableau, which follows the path of the Major Arcana to offer you great insight on different life areas. But more on that later.

My advice is that you do not rush through these practices. Take the time to practice each spread, especially the Nine Card Tableau, which both the 5x5 Tableau and the Major Arcana Tableau build off. I will suggest again that you use a deck you're already comfortable with, as its familiar imagery will facilitate your focus so that you can identify patterns and interactions. If you do not have a deck you feel confident using yet, I suggest the Rider Waite Smith in any of its versions or recolorings.

Now, let's embark on an adventure of discovery with the tableau system.

Chapter 7

Introduction to the Nine Card Tableau

The Nine Card Tableau is like a beautiful, layered painting. It's the ultimate platform on which to build your reading. To get started with the Nine Card Tableau, you will need to lay nine cards in a rectangle. The order in which you lay the cards is irrelevant to the result, though what you see in the graphic is the order that I personally use. For me, it makes sense for the central card to be the first card that is laid, since it is the core of the reading and it represents the root of the situation. This order also allows for the bottom right card, the final outcome card, to be the last card laid on the table. This is personal preference and a habit of mine that you don't need to repeat. If you want to lay the cards starting with the topmost left corner card and pull three cards each to three rows, or in any other way, it will work just the same. See the example on page 66.

Once you have laid the cards, it's time to begin the reading. The tableau is very dynamic, and it has many different layers. This means that, as opposed to positional reading in which you read each card in its individual position before moving to the next, you're going to read the same card(s) multiple times, finding different perspectives as you apply different divination techniques. The beauty of this spread is its flexibility, and there are adjustments that you can make depending on the situation that you are reading on. We'll talk more about that later.

As a final piece of advice before getting started: Eliminate doubt. Stop second-guessing yourself by deciding what you're going to do before you even lay the cards. This will give you clarity and remove any sensation that you may not be "doing it right." Don't decide ahead of time that "this card" means "that outcome." Pull your cards with a timeline in mind. If you are using significators, decide beforehand if you are going to intentionally shuffle them in, or if you are going to see if they come up organically in the reading.

Significator Cards

We have previously discussed significator cards, but now let's dive deeper. In simple terms, a significator card is a card that is given a specific role in the reading. A significator card represents either the querent, a partner, or a person of interest. It can also represent a specific situation. This role is designated by the reader with or without the help of the querent, and it can also appear organically in the reading.

Significator cards can help us have a better understanding of where the querent stands in their situation, what surrounds them, and what is either favorable or unfavorable for them. A significator card can also show us what paths are available, and it can be especially useful when identifying and understanding relational dynamics between two or more people. This comes in handy not just in romantic relationships, but also in complex family dynamics, or even in the workplace. Lastly, a significator card can represent the circumstances that concern the querent, as well as how they will resolve themselves.

While there are numerous pros to using a significator card, there is also a significant con that is worth considering before intentionally incorporating one into your reading. The card takes on a role, an "identity," so to speak, and this role overrides the card's own meaning in the reading. This means that if you choose the Queen of Pentacles as your personal significator in a reading, the Queen of Pentacles now *only* represents you. It shows where you are located in the situation and serves as a map of sorts. This means it will lose any other meaning attached to the card for the duration of the reading. For this reason, it is important to be mindful when using significators.

That being said, significator cards can offer a lot of clarity, especially when identifying relationships and conflicts. The value of knowing exactly where you, or the querent, are located in a particular situation and how to best move forward is very important, so the use of significators can justify the loss of other card meanings if they are incorporated wisely.

Choosing the Right Significator

There are many valid ways to choose a significator. What card you choose can depend on the circumstances, question, or your personal style as a reader. It also depends what kind of significator you want to use. Are you looking for one that represents a specific person? Consider their identity. The significator you choose for your querent will probably be different from one you would choose for their partner or boss. You can also use significators for specific situations. Consider the context. A relationship, a financial issue, a career decision, or spiritual development would also require different significators.

You can choose the method that works for you in general, or what works for you on a case-by-case basis.

Significators and Shuffling

Sometimes it will make sense to intentionally shuffle your significator into the reading. Let's say that you have been asked a question where you've decided it would benefit you as a reader to have an idea of where the querent is located in the situation. If you're using a Nine Card Tableau, you will separate your significator card, shuffle the rest of your deck, pick eight other cards, and shuffle the significator card into those eight cards. Then lay your Nine Card Tableau. If you want to use two significators, you would do the same, and separate those cards first before drawing the remaining seven and shuffling the significator cards into those cards.

Other times, you may decide instead that the first Court Card, if any, to appear in the reading will represent the querent. You can build off this: The first will represent the querent, and the second their partner or another person of interest. The upside of this method is that the cards retain other layers of meaning—for instance, the elemental interactions. You can then make an interpretation based on what does or doesn't come up—remember, what doesn't appear in a reading is every bit as important as what does!

There is also the option of intentionally placing your significator card at the center of the reading instead of shuffling it into the cards. This is not a method that I personally use, since I prefer to see where the card falls on its own, but if it makes sense to you, feel free to do so.

As I always say, the only "requirement" is to be clear about what you're going to do before you draw the cards.

Major Arcana Significator Methods

We've covered the basics of significator cards, so now let's look more deeply into some methods of designating them. How do you know what significator card is right for a querent or a situation?

The first method uses the Major Arcana and is based on personal bonds. This method was passed on to me via word of mouth by a very traditional reader. As a note of caution, this method is gendered and binary in a way that many will find outdated, but it has without a doubt been useful to me in situations regarding family trouble, especially those involving a lot of people. Note, though, that the individual context of the situation will determine the significator cards.

I am passing down this information in the same way that it was passed down to me, many years ago. I encourage you to be flexible with it, adapting it as needed to fit any querent regardless of their gender.

Personal Bonds Major Arcana Method

- **The Magician:** The querent's son/a single male querent/a significantly younger male partner/an illegitimate lover.
- **The High Priestess:** The querent's daughter/a single female querent/a significantly younger female partner/an illegitimate lover.
- **The Empress:** A female querent/the querent's wife or official partner/the querent's mother/the querent's female superior at work.
- **The Emperor:** A male querent/the querent's husband or official partner/the querent's father/the querent's male superior at work.
- **The Hierophant:** A significantly older partner of any gender/a grandfather/an elderly advisor/a teacher or mentor.
- **The Lovers:** Twins/cousins.
- **The Chariot:** An uncle.
- **Strength:** Siblings (other than twins).
- **Temperance:** An aunt.
- **The Star:** A guardian. An aunt or grandmother that fills a mother's role.
- **The Moon:** Grandmother.
- **The Sun:** The querent's children in general.

A simplification of this method that I rely on is to use The Fool/The Empress/The Emperor as significators for the querent (depending on whether or not you want to assign a gender) and, when relevant, to use the counterpart card to represent the querent's partner.

Sun Sign Major Arcana Method

This is a different method that uses the Major Arcana. This time we will take only the querent's astrological sun sign into consideration. You could also use the sun sign of any other relevant individual to whom you are assigning a significator. I am not too keen on this method, because it doesn't leave room for two individuals of the same sun sign to interact, but it is an option that's available.

This method is based on the astrological attributions of each card.

- The Emperor: Aries
- The Hierophant: Taurus
- The Lovers : Gemini
- The Chariot: Cancer
- Strength: Leo
- The Hermit: Virgo
- Justice: Libra
- Death: Scorpio
- Temperance: Sagittarius
- The Devil: Capricorn
- The Star: Aquarius
- The Moon: Pisces

Court Card Significator Methods

There are so many methods that use the Court Cards to choose a significator, based on many different factors. There are even a couple of methods that don't require making a conscious choice. We'll get to those later.

Let's begin with a Court Card method based on the age of the querent or represented party. Again, this method takes the querent's gender into consideration, but remember that there are many ways to be flexible.

Significators Based on Age and Gender: Traditional Spanish Method

This is a method inherited from Spanish cards that has bled into tarot. (Or vice versa.) This method is very binary and lacks flexibility, and while it can be useful in some instances, I do not recommend it as a go-to.

- Kings: Fifty and up, male.
- Kings reversed: Fifty and up, female. (As this method was inherited from Spanish cartomancy, in which there are no Queens, a mature woman is represented by a King, reversed. There are no reversals for the other Court Cards.)
- Queens: Mid-twenties to late forties, female.
- Knights: Mid-twenties to late forties, male.
- Page: Teenager or young adult, usually female but may also be male.

Significators Based on Age and Gender

This is the method that I have encountered more often. It is still binary and not flexible. While it can be a starting point, it leaves out a lot of identities.

- Kings: Mature male.
- Queens: Mature female.
- Knights: Young male.
- Page: Young female/children of any gender.

Significators Based Solely on Age, without Considering Gender

- Kings: Mature or elderly people.
- Queens: Adult.
- Knights: Young adult.
- Pages: Teenager/child.

Significators Based on Personality Types

You can choose to take gender into consideration with this method, or you can use it in a gender-neutral manner. Though it's up to you, using significators in a gender-neutral way has an advantage. You can see how each individual shows up in accordance with the facet of their life that the reading pertains to, and it makes the reading richer, rather than being bound by gender constrictions.

Kings: Usually refers to adult/mature men, but it can refer to a person of any gender that has these characteristics. These are responsible people who have control over themselves and sometimes others. They are grounded and centered.

- King of Swords: The intellectual, witty type. They may be overthinkers. Communicative, sharp, rational, they are stimulated by intellectual challenges and enjoy learning. They usually know a great deal and are fact checkers. Sometimes they can be a bit of the "facts don't care about your feelings" type. They are often academically accomplished and very disciplined.

- King of Wands: The passionate and driven type. They are doers. Their life experience gives them a "been there, done that, got the T-shirt" attitude. They are the go-to person when you're stuck in a rut, simply because they have probably been there too. They are brave. They are risk takers, but at this point in their lives they have learned to take calculated risks. They are very charismatic and sociable.

- King of Cups: The emotionally connected, sensitive type. They don't change easily and have learned to manage their emotions. They have a big heart and often like to help and be hospitable. Usually very creative, they tend to have hobbies they are deeply involved with and that have meaning for them. They tend to have your back and are trustworthy.

- King of Pentacles: The provider type, with a love for stability and predictable life. Usually big family people, they are stubborn and obstinate. They are often financially stable but don't make a display of it, though some can be showy. They tend to have low-key ambitions that have more to do with their own sense of comfort and satisfaction than anything else.

Queens: Usually refers to adult/mature women, although you can of course apply these cards to anyone who fits these descriptions. Grounded and well-centered, they rule over themselves and sometimes others.

- Queen of Swords: The rational and sharp type. They usually have clearly defined boundaries. They tend to be cool-tempered and aren't usually easily agitated. They are communicative and clear, and will not beat around the bush. They can tend to micromanage or want to keep an eye on everything.

- Queen of Wands: The proactive and seductive type. They are independent, lively, and passionate with a tendency to seek adventure. Often difficult to keep up with, they are problem solvers, but they get there through trial and error. Unafraid to take risks and to fail, they are eager to test themselves when necessary.

- Queen of Cups: The intuitive and mothering type. They tend to be caretakers, soft and reliable. They have the ability to walk a mile in someone else's shoes and aren't usually quick to judge. They can be introspective, even if they are known for their ability to make others feel safe and welcome. They have creative tendencies.

- Queen of Pentacles: The protective and domestic type. They value comfort and predictability and are often not too keen on changes. They are good at managing homes, people, and finances, and they are usually excellent when distributing resources and at seeing the potential of a person or situation. They usually assign roles well.

Knights: Younger people of any gender. They are lively, active, and keen on taking risks regardless of the result. They tend to have intense qualities, being less tempered than the more mature Kings and Queens. Knights can have less nuance in their behavior than Queens or Kings. These cards can also refer to older people with immature behaviors.

- Knight of Swords: They speak faster than they think and say what they mean without a filter. They can be passionate defenders of their principles, but they don't take prisoners. In their worst aspects, they can be controlling and sometimes obsessive in their thoughts and actions.

- Knight of Wands: They act faster than they think. They are eager to get things done and tend to be on the run towards the next big thing. They do not rejoice for long in any accomplishment. They are very social people, and infamous seducers.

- Knight of Cups: They feel everything intensely and act before letting those feelings settle. They are in touch with their emotions, to the point where those emotions can override any other consideration. They are likely to make big changes based on temporary feelings, which can lead to regret even if they felt committed at the time.
- Knight of Pentacles: They plan, and plan, and then plan some more! They are slow to act, which makes them likely to be the kind of person who is always stuck in the project phase, never actually progressing. Unlike other knights, they want to be certain before committing to something new.

Pages: These cards usually depict children or teenagers. They can also represent an adult who has a defining negative trait.

- Page of Swords: They are usually introverted children with vivid imaginations. They are intelligent and may be in the advanced class. They defy the limits imposed on them by wanting to experiment. This card may also represent a neurotic adult.
- Page of Wands: They are often mischievous children, the ones who always appear unkempt because they are busy exploring. They are usually very forward and social, and they show signs of leadership from an early age. This card can also represent an audacious or impudent adult.
- Page of Cups: This is the child who doesn't stray far from their parents. They tend to remain close to what is familiar and are not in a rush to explore the outside world. They can be fearful, but they are sweet individuals. This card can represent a very dramatic adult.
- Page of Pentacles: They are quiet and well-mannered children. They like to learn and are usually good students, even if they are not out-of-the-box thinkers like the Page of Swords. This card can also represent a person who is immature, but believes themselves to be the opposite.

Significators Based on Astrological Sun Signs

You can use the astrological correspondence of Court Cards to choose a zodiac-based significator. This option gives you some flexibility if the situation you are reading on involves two people with the same sun sign by using a Page as a placeholder based on the element of that sign.

Air Signs:

- Page of Swords: Any air sign
- Knight of Swords: Aquarius
- Queen of Swords: Libra
- King of Swords: Gemini

Fire Signs:

- Page of Wands: Any fire sign
- Knight of Wands: Leo
- Queen of Wands: Aries
- King of Wands: Sagittarius

Water Signs:

- Page of Cups: Any water sign
- Knight of Cups: Scorpio
- Queen of Cups: Cancer
- King of Cups: Pisces

Earth Signs:

- Page of Pentacles: Any Earth sign
- Knight of Pentacles: Taurus
- Queen of Pentacles: Capricorn
- King of Pentacles: Virgo

My Personal Methods

I have used all these systems at one point or another, and they are all useful. However, as I have evolved as a reader, I developed a tendency towards making things as easy as possible. I'm going to show you the two methods that I use most often and the reasoning behind them.

As a note, I rarely choose a significator and then shuffle it in. I prefer for them to show up naturally in the spread, as whether they show up at all is significant to me.

The first method I use is to begin the reading with the understanding that the first Queen that shows up in the spread (if one shows up at all) will represent a female querent or a partner when relevant to the reading, or someone else who is relevant, and the first King that shows up will represent a male querent or a partner when relevant to the reading, or someone else who is relevant to the reading. I favor this method for readings that involve romantic relationships. I know that this sticks to an outdated and binary conception of gender that does not represent everybody's gender or relationship model. It doesn't have to be Queen = cisgender woman and King = cisgender man. You can ask your querent whether they feel most comfortable with being represented by a Queen or a King regardless of their gender, and when relevant for the reading, it will be the remaining figure that will represent a partner. The card is simply a placeholder for the querent, but we want to make a decision about how they are going to show up beforehand.

You can decide that you want to use Queen + Queen or King + King if the client feels more represented, but the downside to this is that your querent will always appear first in the reading, and that will alter the relationship dynamics since they will always be on top. If you decide that the first King is going to be the querent and the first Queen is going to be their partner, there's a chance that a Queen will show up before a King does.

An alternative use of this method is simply to work with the understanding that the first Queen or King that appears in the spread will represent the querent, regardless of gender, and the second the querent's partner/relevant person in the reading. I favor this method for readings that involve non-romantic relationships.

There is no guarantee that a Queen or King will show up in the reading, let alone two, but, to me, reading cards comes hand in hand with the intrinsic belief that what needs to be on the table will find its way there, and so what is present and what is missing are always relevant.

If there is no significator card, I proceed with the reading. If there is a significator card, I take its position into consideration. If there is a second significator, I consider the relational dynamics between these two cards. If I am reading for a relationship, and the querent or their partner are nowhere to be found in the spread, I take that as a telling aspect of the reading in combination with everything else on the table.

The second method, which I favor for readings that, a priori, don't involve other parties, assumes that the spread itself will tell you who the querent is in the situation, which means that any Court Card that shows up, whether Page, Knight, Queen, or King, will reflect the current state of the querent. For instance, a Page of Cups could speak of a querent who is in the beginning stages of what might bloom into a relationship, or about a querent who is discovering a new creative talent and wondering if it could become their new vocation. Of course, all of this would depend on the context of the reading and the question asked.

In this method, a King would reflect a querent who is coming into the situation with a sense of mastery over it. They feel confident in their ability to navigate the circumstances with a cool head. A Queen would reflect a querent who comes into the situation with a desire to nourish, exercising a more passive form of power, or contributing to the situation through their actions. A Knight would speak of a querent who comes into the situation ready and eager to act. Lastly, a Page would describe a querent who comes into the situation without prior experience, ready to learn but not at a point in which they feel confident.

Situational Significators

Situational significators are much more flexible than ones used to represent a querent or a specific person in the reading. Don't worry about the Major Arcana, Minor Arcana, or Court Cards here. Any card that represents the issue can be chosen. This significator can represent either the problem or the desired result, depending on how the question is asked. For instance, if the question is "Will my difficult financial situation improve?" the significator could be the Five of Pentacles. However, if the question is phrased "How can I achieve financial stability for myself and mine?" the significator could be the Ten of Pentacles instead.

Your situational significator should match the subject of the reading. While getting *just* the right nuance of meaning to precisely describe your problem is not necessary, as the card is just a placeholder, it is my recommendation that you choose the closest thing. This way you're not missing out on any other meaning by choosing a card that could add to the reading. I believe that the cards have a way of getting the message through even if something is missing. (I have done successful readings and then realized later that one or more cards had been accidentally left out of the box or bag.)

While this is not an extensive list, here are a few of my situational significators to give you a jumping-off point.

Romance Matters

- Unexpected breakup: Three of Swords
- Expected breakup: Five of Cups
- Necessary breakup: Eight of Cups
- Situationship: The Hanged Man
- Lack of communication: Four of Swords
- Relationship (When will a new one appear?): The Lovers or Two of Cups
- Stable relationship: The Lovers or Two of Cups
- Infidelity (Querent wondering how to get away with it): Seven of Swords
- Infidelity (Querent on the receiving end): Temperance. Temperance can be an infidelity card in the right context. It is a very non-committal card, and in its traditional representation in the Rider Waite Smith, the figure is depicted with one foot in the water and the other on the ground. You want to pay special attention to what cards lie on each foot of Temperance, that is, directly below it and in the bottom right diagonal. If you have two people cards there, or other cards that point towards infidelity or secrets, that can be an indication.

Career Matters

- Promotion: Six of Wands
- Restructuring: The Tower

- Layoffs: Death/Five of Pentacles
- Work stability: Eight of Pentacles
- Entrepreneurship (solo): The Magician
- Interview: Ace of Swords

Financial Matters

- General wealth: The Wheel of Fortune
- Inheritance: Ten of Pentacles
- Savings: Four of Pentacles
- Investments: Seven of Pentacles
- Donations: Six of Pentacles
- Dire finances: Five of Pentacles

Spiritual Matters

- Spiritual awakening: Judgement
- New spiritual path: The Fool
- Organized religion: The Hierophant
- Non-organized religion: The High Priestess
- Solo spiritual practice: The Hermit
- Specific deity work: Choose a fitting Court Card to represent the specific deity. If you're unsure, the Emperor or Empress also works. Some Major Arcana have been traditionally connected with certain deities, so you can use those if you're familiar with them.
- House of worship: The Tower

Non-Romantic Relationship Matters

- Friendship: Three of Cups
- Colleague competitiveness: Five of Swords

- Family trouble: Use the significators from the Personal Bonds Major Arcana Method section. For a particularly tumultuous family life in general, especially if the family lives together, use The Tower to represent the physical house.
- Gaslighting (querent on the receiving end): Two of Swords
- Emotional blackmail: Eight of Swords

Health Matters

- Pain: Ten of Swords
- Exhaustion: Ten of Wands
- Insomnia: Nine of Swords
- Suspected illness: The Moon

How to Use Situational Significators

There are three different methods you can use with situational significators. In the first method, select your significator and place it at the center of the spread. You'll then draw another eight cards to surround it if you are using the Nine Card Tableau, or another twenty-four cards if you are using the 5x5 Tableau. This puts the situational significator card at the core of the reading, with the rest of the spread revolving around it, and gives you the option to see all the interactions with it at the center.

An alternative approach is to select your significator first, draw the rest of the cards for your spread, and then shuffle in your significator. Lay the spread and see what position your significator card naturally falls into. This can provide insight into other aspects of the reading, especially when taking into account where it falls timeline-wise. For now, hold on to this information and we will see more about the timeline later. Whether the significator falls in the past, present, or future is a valuable piece of information. Does the situation have an impact in the present? Is it something dragged in from the past? Or is it a fear for the future, a looming threat that may not come to pass?

The last option is to mentally assign a significator but not do anything to intentionally include it in the drawn cards. Simply work with the assumption that if the card that represents the situation naturally makes its way into the spread, then it is something that requires special attention. If the card doesn't appear, take it to mean that you can consider other possibilities, or that the situation may not be quite what you anticipated.

Each method is useful for different situations and all are valid. Remember that including a significator is completely optional. It's simply one of the tools available to enhance your readings. While significators can add an interesting interpretative layer, make sure that you are enhancing the reading when employing a technique, and not making it more difficult by adding unnecessary frills.

The Relational Dynamics in the Tableau

The position of the cards can say a lot about the existing relationships between people. It can speak to their degree of closeness and the conflicts between them. The elemental interaction between these cards is added to this interpretation, including a layer of compatibility.

There are different dimensions to this. We have seen the dimension of power, which is defined by the position of the cards in relation to one another vertically. Now, we are going to explore connections based on whether the cards are facing each other, opposing one another, or showing their backs to each other.

Cards that face each other are in agreement, at least the majority of the time. These cards are on the same team and there is collaboration between them. In the odd instances in which two cards that face one another are in conflict, this will be an open conflict with direct hostilities in which no party is pretending otherwise. To know if there is a conflict between two cards that are facing each other, look at the surrounding cards and especially at the card in between them.

Distance also plays a role here. Two cards that face one another and that fall in the same row with no other card between them are the closest. This position indicates a supportive relationship, perhaps even with one or both parties acting as the other's confidant. When the cards are in the same row but with a card in between them, that card can be a common goal or a barrier between them, depending on the situation and context. If the cards are facing one another but in different rows, the power dynamics also play a role in the interpretation.

Cards that are back-to-back are in disagreement or disconnected. They have different focuses, and they are not rowing in the same direction. This can indicate a conflict, but it can also simply indicate that these individuals are not taking one another into consideration. For instance, in the context of a long-term relationship, back-to-back partners could indicate a disconnection or different priorities. In the context of a new romantic interest, the same position can indicate that they are not on the same page about what the connection entails. As with the previous positions, the closer they are, the more significant the disagreement or conflict. When two cards are together but back-to-back, there may be intense feelings of disagreement, but they are still close. The greater the distance, the greater the disconnect, and the less likelihood there is of turning it around.

A card that "chases" another—that is to say, when a card faces another card that is showing its back to it—indicates a person who is trying to connect with someone who is unavailable, disinterested, or disdainful. The greater the distance, the less likelihood there is to get that person's attention.

Checklist

- Look at the proximity between significators: How close or far away from each other are they? Are there connecting, conflicting, neutral, or isolating cards between them?
- Location: Are they in the same row? In opposing corners? In the same column? What is their vertical relationship like?
- Body language: Are they face-to-face? Back-to-back? Is someone showing their back to another?

Timeline

The timeline of the reading will help us get situated and grant us insight into the development of the situation. Not all questions require the same timeline, so deciding your timeline beforehand is helpful.

The standard timeline that I use on most occasions is a past—present—future outline. Each moment in time is represented by a row of three cards. The top row represents the past or the foundation of the situation. It shows us how the situation came to be. The central row represents the present, the current situation and its immediate developments, highlighting the querent's current position. The bottom row represents the future, where things are heading or how the matter will be resolved, and it shows the options available to the querent.

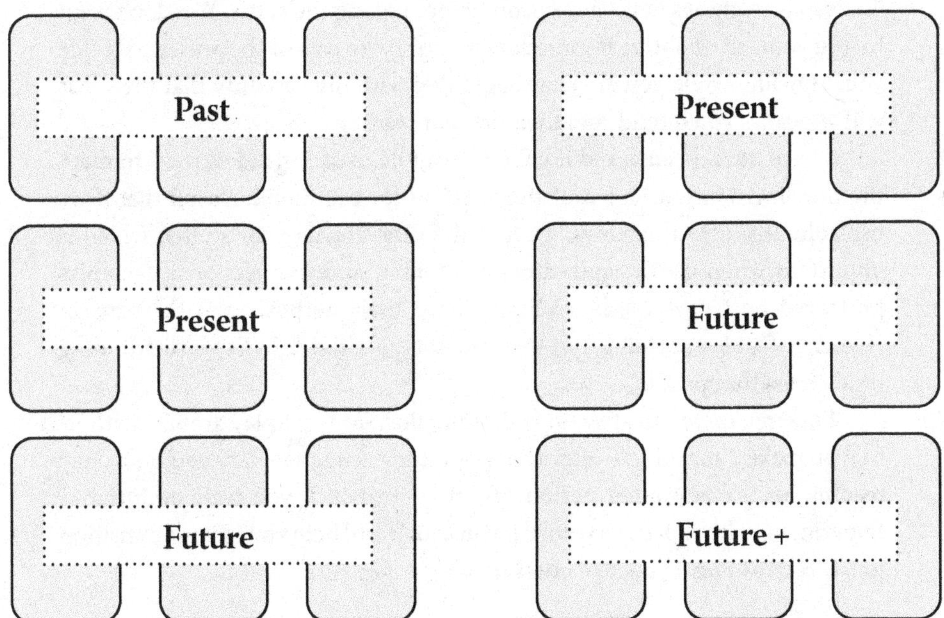

This is a very versatile timeline. Sometimes, even if the reading is purely predictive, I still like to use the past—present—future layout simply because I like to have information about the timeline of the situation. Even if the querent doesn't care to hear about the past, it can still be incredibly useful for us as readers to get that background from the cards.

There are other options when it comes to timelines, though. If the matter is purely predictive and there is no interest whatsoever in digging into the past, or if it is a situation that has developed so recently that looking into its past is essentially pointless, there is the option to begin the reading with the present in the top row. This still offers some orientation about where the querent is in the current affairs. You can then use the two other rows to expand further and further into the future, getting a good sense of what the querent can expect moving forward.

A different way to use the timeline is to divide a set period of time between the rows. For a week-ahead reading, for instance, the top row can speak about the first part of the week, the central row about the middle of the week, and the bottom row about the end of the week. The distribution can work similarly when looking a month ahead. For longer periods of time, I suggest using a larger spread, such as the 5x5 Tableau.

My advice when it comes to choosing a timeline for your Nine Card Tableau is to always make a decision before pulling the cards. You don't want to find yourself doubting if something refers to the past or the present. Decide your timeline while you are shuffling, filled with the certainty that the cards will appear as you intend, and then do your reading.

I have often been asked if columns can be used instead of rows to mark the timeline. I am not a fan of this method for the simple reason that if we use columns instead of rows, we lose the directionality rows offer, which is important when using significators or looking into the relational dynamics portrayed by Court Cards. Columns have their purpose, and they are an element of tableau reading, but they are not quite the right fit for distributing time across the spread.

Feel free to get creative with the timeline. You can play around with it! Maybe make a morning—afternoon—evening timeline when you do a daily reading, or use any other period of time with which you feel comfortable. Experiment with it! Keep a record if you can. It will help you in your transition to tableau reading if you take notes on your experiences.

The Spine of the Tableau

The "spine" of the tableau refers to the three cards that sustain the reading. These are the top left card, the card at the center of the spread, and the card on the bottom right.

The role of these cards is to give, at a glance, an overall idea of the situation you are reading on and its development. These cards give us a good baseline of information, and each has its own role.

The top left card adds a nuance to the reading, a "flavor" of sorts. The Sun in this placement would add optimism to the reading. It would perhaps soften the meaning of the other cards a bit, or at least leave some room for hope. It may indicate a good outcome, even if it is not the desired one. The Ten of Swords in this placement would add an air of despair and pain to the reading. The rest of the cards would be tinted with that energy. The Eight of Wands would add an energetic quality to the reading, suggesting an element of speed or even haste. It would indicate that all of the querent's focus is on the situation at this time.

The central card shows the core element of the reading. This is what is at the heart of the matter. The central card indicates what the reading is truly about, or what it is rooted in. In a general reading, it can show us what brought the querent to the table. A Court Card in this position would indicate that the situation is focused on the person, or on the energy that the card represents. The Hermit in this position would suggest that, at its core, the situation revolves around an inner perception. The Ten of Pentacles would suggest that the situation is a long-term one, or that it revolves around matters that will affect the querent for a long time to come. This, of course, changes according to the context of each reading.

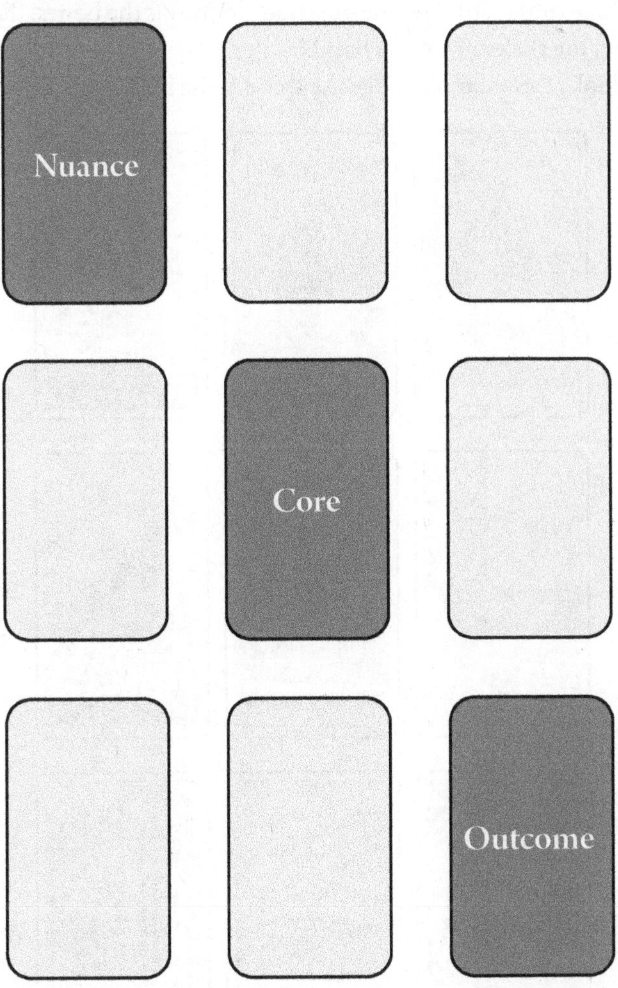

The bottom right card is the strongest outcome card. It has the most weight when it comes to determining whether we can expect an outcome that is favorable or unfavorable in this situation. If we found the Two of Pentacles in this position, then at first glance we could conclude that the matter will remain up in the air, that it will not be sorted in the foreseeable future, or it will remain unstable. The Four of Wands on the other hand, would suggest a stable resolution.

Looking at these three cards, we can get a general idea of what to expect. Pay attention to how these cards interact with the question at hand: Do they seem to support it? Do they seem to oppose it? Are those the cards that you would expect to see in the situation that you're reading about? The interaction between these three cards and the question/context is the bones, the spine, of our reading, the skeleton we will build on.

Let's look at an example to see the spine of the reading in action.

Question: "What are Tiffany's prospects at her new job?"

Since this reading is entirely predictive, and Tiffany's position is new, it wouldn't make sense to use a timeline with a past. The timeline we're using instead is present—immediate future—longer term future.

Nuance card (top left): The Queen of Cups. We can understand this spread from the perspective of a woman for whom finding meaning and having an emotional involvement in what she does for a living is important.

Core card (center): Justice. In the context of a new position at work, Justice can be understood as a fairness between what goes in and what comes out, a balance of effort and reward. This card is also clinical. Justice is not emotional, but rather determined by a series of rules. It can indicate a certain coldness in the situation, especially considering that its placement is close to cards that don't bring the most positive aspect to the reading.

Outcome card (bottom right): The Nine of Wands. This situation seems to lead to a tiring outcome. While the querent has what it takes to persevere in her new position, it is a task that requires effort and that doesn't seem to grant much in terms of satisfaction.

These three cards are enough to set a tone for the reading. We know about the energy that the querent is putting into her new position, we see the emergence of a key theme for her, and we know that things are likely to become more difficult than anticipated.

Rows

Now that we know the general tone of our reading, let's return to the timeline. It is time to interpret each row of our spread for Tiffany's new position. In this case, the top row will speak about the starting point of the situation. Since we are dealing with a new job, the start of the job would be our beginning.

This top row is all water: Queen of Cups—Five of Cups—Four of Cups. It is interesting to note that the cards are following a decreasing pattern and that water doesn't appear again in the reading. Considering that the Queen of Cups is the nuance card and highlights the importance of feeling that the job has meaning, we can see a disappointment in that regard with the Five of Cups, which turns into a certain indifference with the Four of Cups that follows.

The job will soon lose its luster and Tiffany will lose, or is already losing, the motivation to be engaged with it.

The central row moves into the future and shows how the situation will develop. In this case, we have The Wheel of Fortune—Justice—Seven of Wands. Considering how the querent's attitude has deflated in the first row, we can see that The Wheel of Fortune with Justice is neutral. This combination points to an inertia. However, the Seven of Wands suggests that there is a resistance to it. It probably won't feel natural for Tiffany to get sucked into this day-to-day routine where there is no meaning for her, even though the environment doesn't seem to be negative in itself. There is a fairness to the company or in her position. That sense of fairness, of being in an environment that doesn't push employees past their job descriptions, can be an incentive for her when thinking about the job. She will be at odds with her more reasonable self when she must confront how she truly feels about the matter.

The third row is the outcome row, and it moves further ahead in the future, speaking about longer-term developments for Tiffany. We have the Ten of Pentacles—Eight of Wands—Nine of Wands. It is worth noting that there's an ascendent sequence from the Seven of Wands, to the Eight of Wands, to the Nine of Wands. This seems to suggest that the initial resistance may develop *in crescendo* for the querent. The Ten of Pentacles speaks of a situation that offers stability, and that can be a reason to hold on to the job. However, it is not the kind of motivation that the querent is looking for and, while it can work for a time with the Eight of Wands, the situation comes to a point in which the querent is holding onto their position, yes, but is not happy about it, as the Nine of Wands suggests.

Columns

The columns offer additional information to substantiate our interpretation. On many occasions, they merely repeat information. This is not a bad thing. It simply means that there are different ways to come to the same conclusion in the reading, which reinforces that interpretation. Other times, though, the columns add some interesting insight to the interpretation. This is especially true when there are significator cards involved and the columns either add to the dynamic reflected in the reading or give more substance to the represented individual's behavior.

In the case of Tiffany's new position, the columns do not provide a lot of new information, but let's go through them anyway just to show you how it's done.

The first column is the Queen of Cups, The Wheel of Fortune, and the Ten of Pentacles. We can see how, directionally, the Queen is facing away from the spread, and The Wheel of Fortune below her keeps Tiffany going back and forth between her search for meaning in her career and the stability offered by the Ten of Pentacles.

The second column, with the Five of Cups, Justice, and Eight of Wands, depicts a similar inner conflict. The train of thought may be something like, "What is there to complain about, really?" This makes Tiffany feel that, when she is looking at the situation objectively and focusing on the positives, there may not be a lot to cry about. And yet, those feelings of needing a purpose remain there, at the forefront of the matter.

The third column, with the Four of Cups, Seven of Wands, and Nine of Wands, shows us how Tiffany's indifference towards the position will turn into resistance and, likely, ultimately into a burnout.

Corners

The role of the corners in tableau reading offers another new layer of insight. As with the other methods, it can sometimes be redundant. But sometimes it can be extremely insightful. Everything depends on the specific reading, the context of the question, and the cards that make it onto the table. There are times when the answer is obvious, and there are times when it is necessary to dig a little bit deeper to come to a conclusion.

The top corners are the first and third cards in the top row. They are an external influence on the situation that is shown at the core. That is to say, they show factors that are influencing the main issue.

The bottom corners are the first and third cards in the bottom row. They are the areas which can be influenced *by* the situation at the core. That is to say, they offer options that we can influence from our present.

In our reading on Tiffany's new position, we can see how the Queen of Cups and the Four of Cups are influencing Justice. These are two water cards. One is a water card that embodies a nourishing and involved spirit, and the other one embodies apathy and disengagement. Both of these are affecting the objectivity of the situation, which is represented by Justice. Yes, looking at the matter from a detached perspective, the job isn't bad at all, but the need for meaning and the fact that we don't find it in the reading will end up having a significant role no matter what.

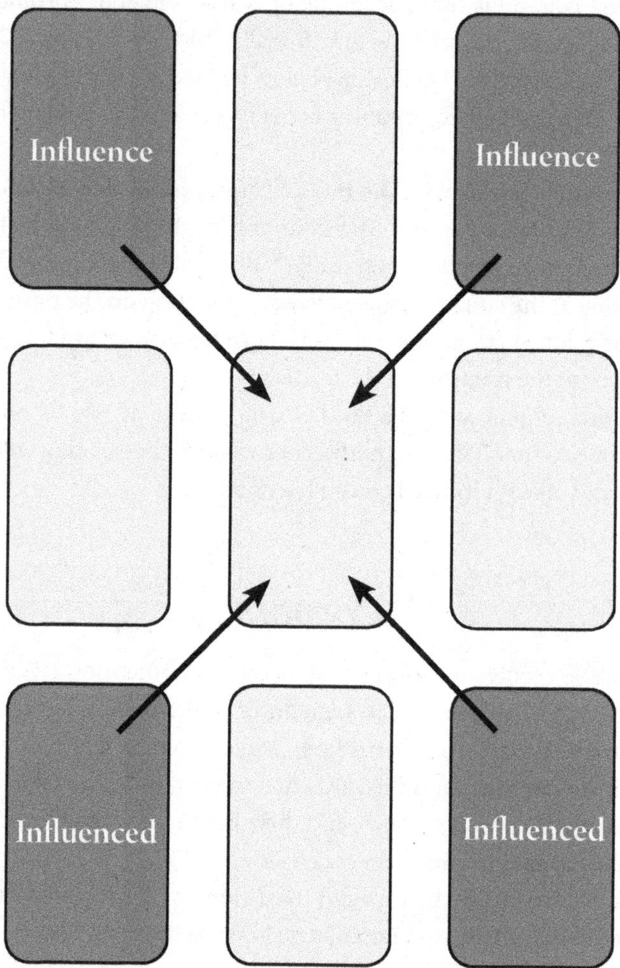

The Ten of Pentacles and the Nine of Wands can be influenced by a rational perspective as shown by Justice. Tiffany can absolutely make a choice to make the best out of the positive aspects that the situation offers. She could rest in the long-term potential of the position and make it a means to an end career move. This is reflected in the pure spirit of resilience shown in the Nine of Wands, but with the price of not having that sense of genuine engagement with it.

Knighting

Knighting is a tableau technique that has a reputation for creating a lot of confusion. Don't worry! It's simple once you get the hang of it.

Knighting traces its origin to the movement of the Knight in chess. It involves connecting two cards through an "L" movement. This might be two cards up or down and one to the left or right, or two to the left or right and one up or down. If you are familiar with Lenormand, then you may already be familiar with the technique. You may even think that this is solely a Lenormand technique. While it is a cartomantic technique that is often associated with Lenormand, it is not exclusive to it. This is how it works:

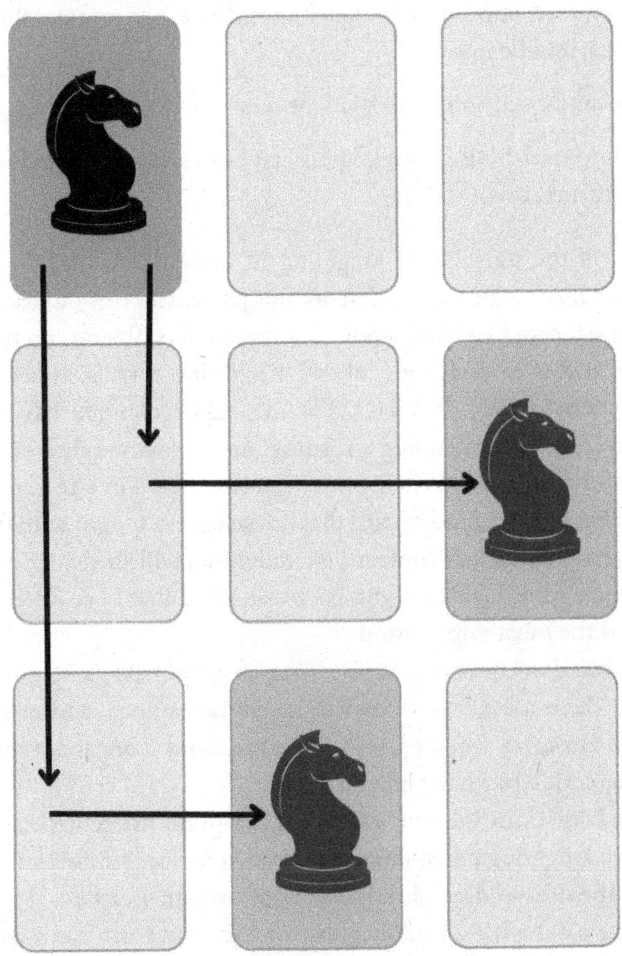

- First card, top row knights third card, middle row and second card, bottom row.
- Second card, top row knights first and third, bottom row.
- Third card, top row knights first card, middle row and second card, bottom row.
- First card, middle row knights third card, top row and third card, bottom row.
- Third card, middle row knights first card, top row and first card, bottom row.
- First card, bottom row knights second card, top row and third card, middle row.
- Second card, bottom row knights first and third cards, top row.
- Third card, bottom row knights first card, second row and second card, first row.

What is the purpose of knighting in tableau reading? Because this technique connects two cards that are not physically close to each other in the reading, it reveals a connection that may be less obvious on the surface. It usually shows underlying motives. Knighting reveals hidden feelings, concerns, convictions, or values. For me, this technique has often held the key to truly understanding a reading, or to making sense of cards that initially left me puzzled. When you encounter a card in a reading that you don't understand, the kind of card that doesn't seem to "go" with the rest, or when you have cards that confuse you, knighting will shed a lot of light and provide you with valuable insight. It's a technique that I use often and that I find reveals the most information.

Now, you don't have to interpret every single possible knighting between the cards. There are a lot of possible knighting options, and many will be redundant. However, when you want to understand more about the role of a card, pay attention to what it knights.

In the Nine Card Tableau, every card except for the central card is going to have two knighting possibilities. The card at the center doesn't knight any other, but the surrounding cards each knight two other cards.

To figure out what a card knights, you can count two cards down or up and one left or right, or one card up or down and one card left or right. If you find you're struggling to do this visually, try the practical exercise with a game piece or coin until the motion feels natural and easy for you.

Let's go back to our reading on Tiffany's new position. The Queen of Cups knights the Seven of Wands (two to the right, one down) and the Eight of Wands (one to the right, two down).

The Five of Cups knights the Ten of Pentacles (two down, one left) and the Nine of Wands (two down, one right).

The Wheel of Fortune knights the Four of Cups (two right, one up) and the Nine of Wands (two right, one down).

What do these combinations tell us?

The Queen of Cups knighting the Seven of Wands and the Eight of Wands can point to an inner struggle between the reluctancy to stay in the position and the desire to focus on it. The Five of Cups knighting the Ten of Pentacles and the Nine of Wands ties the decision to stay with the company long-term to disappointment and to a grieving process, the acceptance of the fact that this position will not bring inner satisfaction. The Wheel of Fortune knighting the Four of Cups and the Nine of Wands suggests an ongoing back-and-forth between a sense of duty and a sense of apathy.

Bridging

Bridging is a technique where two cards in the same horizontal row are separated by a middle card. It is a connecting technique that identifies what stands between two energies, or what holds two energies together. This is a particularly useful technique to use when people cards, which are Court Cards, or any other card that's acting as a person in the reading, are involved, as we will see later, but it is also useful when we want to know what "glues" a set of circumstances together, or when we need to uncover an obstacle that prevents two desirable energies from merging.

While the Tiffany reading doesn't provide the best example of bridging, the last row gives us an idea of how it works: Nothing in the spread seems to indicate that Tiffany, as uncomfortable as she might be, will take the step to leave her job in the foreseeable future. What holds the Ten of Pentacles and the Nine of Wands together? The focused energy of the Eight of Swords, which takes a "let's get the job done" perspective.

A different way of understanding bridging is with the characters in the cards. Examine this sample reading.

The Queen and King are back-to-back, so we can read this as a situation in which there is conflict. They are not seeing eye to eye. What stands in between them? The Five of Wands: open conflicts, arguments, and maybe chaos, the inability to agree on something.

Chapter 8

Power Dynamics in the Tableau

Power dynamics are the interactions between two or more cards that represent people. As previously stated, these are usually Court Cards, though occasionally other cards may represent the querent and other significant people in the reading.

To read on these power dynamics, let's take into consideration a few different factors. Are the cards facing each other? How have the people cards landed in the reading? Are they present in the same or different rows? We also need to consider the ranks, in case of the Court Cards, and the cards they are surrounded by.

Let's explore the power dynamics that exist among the Court Cards. These can act as a reflection of the power dynamics between people in family environments, romantic relationships, or the workplace. Let's ground our interpretation by looking at the roles of the Court Cards in their historical context.

Pages are assistants. They are usually in the lower ranks of power dynamics, with a few exceptions. Pages, historically, were in the service of everyone who was superior in rank, so they had less power than knights, queens, and kings. However, one of the "perks" of being in service of another is that it made these pages privy to intimate information. It also granted them knowledge of the character of the person to whom they were tending.

When a Page exerts their power, it's usually in an underhanded or subtle way, either through manipulation or blackmail. The Page must always keep in mind that their more powerful counterpart often has the means to crush their attempt. When we are in a Page situation, the power that is available for us to leverage is personal information, but we risk being silenced by someone who is more openly powerful than we are.

Knights are in an intermediate position. They were usually members of the gentry who did the bidding of the king. It was important that both parties be in harmony with one another, as it was in the king's best interest to avoid having the knights turn against him. At the same time, the king wanted to remind the knights who was in charge. Being an "executive" force of sorts, the knight's power is in knowing that they are necessary, but not irreplaceable. In addition, the "shelf life" of a knight was not excessively long. Accumulating merits to be not just in the king's good books, but also in his debt, was an intelligent move.

When we are in a Knight situation, our power resides in knowing what we bring to the table, and that we can withdraw it. At the same time, we have to be okay with the risk that someone else may arrive and provide the same things.

Queens and kings hold a different kind of power, one that is intertwined. While traditionally the king is considered the one with the utmost power, he needs a queen to ensure that power continues. Without the queen, the king cannot strengthen his line. The king might be on top of the power pyramid, but it is the queen who makes sure that he remains there. Strengthening his line is how she gains power, but failing to do so is how she loses it.

The queen, then, has a passive power that is subject to the fulfillment of a role. Once fulfilled, though, her position is fairly strong. The king, on the other hand, has a more overt kind of power. He doesn't need to go down the route of intrigue and he can command in a more open way. With that said, his privilege grants him a lot of benefits, but also speaks of obligations to fulfill.

Considering these dynamics, the Queen and King cards can be seen as equal partners when positively aspected, but when their positions or surrounding cards suggest a more negative aspect, it can speak to a power struggle. A Queen or King that has one or more Knights or Pages above them can speak of an individual incapable of wielding their power, whether that's a manager who doesn't know how to lead or who isn't taken seriously, a parent who is being undermined by a child, or a querent who is giving too much attention to people who are not there to stay. The reason why we usually pick a Queen or King as a significator is because they have that "main character" energy about themselves.

In general, Kings and Queens will be above Knights and Pages, with the latter being the last in rank.

Another complementary way of identifying the power dynamics of a relationship is the position of the cards in the tableau in reference to one another. When two characters are in the same row, they are on the same level, and they are either equally invested in the situation or they have a similar rank. In the context of a new romantic interest, this could translate into a situation in which there is no power play. Both parties stand on even footing, though whether the figures on the cards are facing one another will give us additional information. In an established relationship, it speaks of a relationship of equals. With a career question, this placement may say that both coworkers are on the same level, or, if they are in different ranks, then they are at least not trying to overpower each other.

When one character is on top of another, that is a sign of dominance over a situation. The dominant person is holding the pan by the handle, so to speak. The closer the cards are, the stronger the dominance.

If we focus exclusively on the Court Cards in this spread, we can see that there are two kings, the King of Swords and the King of Wands, who appear in the same row. They are also facing one another. This suggests a relationship in which they are on the same level. The card in between them, the Five of Cups, represents what they are focused on. The Five of Cups may indicate that they are facing a loss or a disappointment that affects them both. There is a third figure, however, in the Knight of Swords. He is below the Kings. The position of the Knight with respect to the Kings suggests that they hold a position of shared power over the Knight. The Kings, for example, may represent managers while the knight is an employee, or teachers and a student, or parents and a child. The Knight of Swords has a better disposition towards the King of Swords than towards the King of Wands, though he is influenced by both.

These are all things to keep in mind when reading on power dynamics. Consider the figures in the cards, the directions in which they're facing, and the relationship they have not just to each other but also to the situation.

Directionality

Directionality is important in any style of reading, but even more so in the tableau. Most cards have a directional component in one way or another. In the Rider Waite Smith, the hand in the Ace of Wands comes from the right, which suggests that it has an impact on the left, but the hand in the Ace of Swords comes from the left. The figure in the Nine of Wands seems to be wary of a threat that comes from the left side, while the man in the Eight of Swords walks to the right side, and the figures in the Six of Wands, Seven of Swords, and Eight of Cups travel in the same direction. The Magician points, his arms a diagonal line, to above and below, and the Seven of Swords walks towards the left but looks to the right.

These details in the cards' movement can deepen the interpretation. Consider the position of the Six of Swords, for example. Is it on the right column, exiting the spread? This position would provide information about what is left behind. If it is on the left, we would instead focus on where that movement is heading. Death has a trail of corpses in the background, which suggests that the situation or circumstances behind Death have already ended, but what is in front of Death is also about to end. What card is to the left of the Four of Cups, where the fourth cup is being offered? That may be a hint towards what's being ignored.

While these examples are based on the Rider Waite Smith, you can apply them to any deck. Take this directionality into consideration in your readings, using it to acquire more information and add depth.

Here is a simple example of the importance of directionality. Let's look at two different combinations of the same three cards.

On the left side, the figure in the Eight of Swords is leaving behind an emotionally difficult situation or heartbreak. Perhaps they are overcoming a breakup, which presents the opportunity of a new option offered by the Ace of Cups. On the right side, the order is inverted, thus the meaning is altered. The Ace of Cups comes from the right and is followed by the Eight of Cups, suggesting that this querent made an offer of love, one that was probably unrequited. They are leaving that situation behind, as they are now walking towards the Eight of Swords.

In the first option, the Ace of Cups is an offer made to the querent, an opportunity that they are on the receiving end of, while in the second option they are the one who made the offer.

Reading the Tableau: A Practical Example

Having explored tableau reading and its multiple techniques, it's time to see how it works in action. We're going to look at two different examples, with some exercises along the way to give you the opportunity to practice.

My advice is that you take time to examine the different spreads. Try to answer the questions yourself before you read my interpretation. Explore how your interpretation differs from mine, as well as when we came to similar conclusions. Remember to pay attention to the different layers of interpretation available to you.

Example #1

Our querent, Oscar, wants to know his career prospects for the next six months. Considering that this is an entirely predictive reading, the timeline I've chosen for this spread starts in the present with the top row and moves further into the future to look into the next six months. This is a preferable timeline for this reading.

Exercise questions:

- Does the reading clearly indicate career progression?
- Does the reading have a consistent flow or are there abrupt changes?
- Do you notice any interesting patterns?

Step-by-step interpretation: The Six of Wands in the nuance position is a vigorous way to start the reading, suggesting that Oscar brings a drive to conquer career goals over the next few months. The Eight of Pentacles at the core position indicates Oscar's professional development and a desire to master his skills, which suggests that he's comfortable in his current occupation. He's not thinking about switching jobs within the timeframe given. The Two of Swords in the outcome position, though, suggests that there is a missing piece of information, or a reality that the querent may not be taking into consideration that keeps him stuck in the current situation.

Let's look at the elemental disposition of the reading:

- We have three fire cards: The Six of Wands, The Wheel of Fortune, and Temperance.
- We have three air cards: The Four of Swords, the Six of Swords, and the Two of Swords.
- We have two earth cards: The Empress and the Eight of Pentacles.
- We have one water card: The Three of Cups.

The main conflict on an elemental level is between fire and air. The Six of Wands and The Wheel of Fortune gain traction, which is suddenly stopped by the Four of Swords. Temperance and The Six of Swords are a positive interaction between fire and air. This interaction revives the fire, but again that traction is stopped by the Two of Swords.

There are positive interactions in the second row between earth and water. Promising seeds are being planted. However, it's also true that the elements that are interacting positively, water and earth, are slow ones. These elemental interactions suggest that progress will not be fast, but that steps towards future career progression will be taken within the next six months.

Let's look at the numerological aspect. Seven out of nine cards are even numbers, with the only one odd number repeating: The Empress, the third card of the Major Arcana, and the Three of Cups. There is also a repetition of sixes, with the Six of Wands and the Six of Swords. These are cards that share a "moving forward" type of energy. With three being a repeating number of expansion and six being a repeating number that foretells harmony, in conjunction with the majority of even numbers, it can be concluded that while Oscar may not find the kind of progress that he was aiming for within the given timeframe, he can count on career stability and his position is not at risk.

Let's investigate the rows now. First row: Six of Wands, The Wheel of Fortune, Four of Swords. This trio suggests that the querent comes from a place in which there was a recent win and he's hoping that this energy will generate some momentum. The Four of Swords, though, seems to dissolve that buildup, and Oscar may be disappointed by the lack of immediate improvement after his conquest.

Second row: The Empress, Eight of Pentacles, Three of Cups. This row indicates that Oscar is well-integrated in his workplace and will remain so. It is possible, though, that this is problematic for his immediate development. The Empress and the Eight of Pentacles suggest some expertise on Oscar's side, a seniority that is worth some further recognition. The Three of Cups signifies that he is integrated with his team and enjoys fruitful social relationships. He is considered an excellent employee and team player. The card indicates that his performance is satisfactory; however, the lack of progression in the previous card may point towards Oscar doing *too* well in his current position, so much so that it is not in his company's best interest to move him to a different position or offer him a more tangible recognition.

Third row: Temperance, The Six of Swords, and the Two of Swords reinforce the idea of a long wait. Temperance suggests patience, but it's also a pretty noncomital card by itself. Together with the Six of Swords and the Two of Swords, it can speak of empty promises of growth that do not come to pass within the required timeframe.

Let's knight a few key cards to uncover what hinders Oscar's progress. I've decided to knight the Two of Swords because I want to know what Oscar is missing in this situation. The Two of Swords knights to The Empress and The Wheel of Fortune, two cards that are big on timing. This suggests that progress won't come just yet. At the same time, the two cards are positive enough in the context to allow us to interpret that progress *will* come, but that Oscar is blinded when it comes to a realistic timeline, which keeps him in the dark. This could end up being a source of resentment down the line.

I also wanted to knight the Four of Swords. Since the Four and the Two are the most opposing cards in the spread, I thought it would be useful to see what's behind this card. The Four of Swords knights The Empress and the Six of Swords. This seems to confirm that the inactivity of the four can turn into the movement of the six, but it will not happen within the given timeframe.

So, having gone through a few techniques, let's return to the question to see the answer.

"What are Oscar's career prospects for the next six months?"

The next six months of Oscar's career look stable, without any concerning threats. A recent or a soon-to-come achievement will seem to bring him a sense of upward momentum. However, it will not result in any tangible improvement regarding Oscar's current career. His performance will remain strong and so will the appreciation of his team, but his integration in his department can work against his desire for progress, having become a worker that his teammates may overly rely on. While there are indicators that, in due course, there will be rewards for his current efforts, he may not want to take promises of progress too seriously, since the company could be dragging its feet when it comes to delivering. There will be opportunities to plant seeds for growth during this period, but they will bloom further along the way.

Example #2

Julian owns a growing business together with a partner. They are planning to open a second location, but Julian wants to know if it would be better to open it in a different city or if a local option is better.

Exercise questions:

- What are the relational dynamics?
- Is there unanimity or are there two distinct opinions clashing?
- Is a different city or the same city the better option?

The layout is on page 104.

Step-by-step interpretation: Let's begin with the nuance card, the core, and the outcome card. The Three of Wands in the nuance position (the top left card) confirms that, whatever happens, both partners have the expansion of the business in mind. Regardless of where, there will be a second location for their business. Uncertainty is at the core with the Two of Pentacles. They want to make the best decision and grow the business, of course, but they also want to make sure that they can juggle both locations, so comfortable management is at the core of the spread. The Six of Wands as an outcome seems to paint an optimistic picture and indicates that the expansion of the business will be done successfully.

Relational dynamics and significators: It's important to stop and take note of the relational dynamics of the situation, considering that there are two Court Cards present. Following my own method when choosing a significator, the first Court Card, the Knight of Wands, represents Julian, while the King of Swords represents his partner. They are facing one another, which is a good sign of getting along with each other as business partners. Elementally, they are fire and air. Julian is the doer, the one who is ready to make things happen and figure out on the go. His partner brings in a more balanced approach and prefers to take facts into consideration. Julian's ready-to-go attitude can push his partner into action, but sometimes his partner's air can be enough to tamp down Julian's fire.

In the situation we're reading on, Julian may be feeling more strongly about expanding the business to a location further away, considering that The Chariot and the Three of Wands are in his line of sight. His partner, on the other hand, has doubts about the idea, and he wants to make sure that they have what's necessary to successfully be on top of both locations.

When looking at the cards that surround each significator, we can see that The Chariot is auspicious to the Knight of Wands, so Julian's idea seems to be favorable to the venture. Sitting on top of The Magician, he feels convinced of their ability to be on top of both locations without issue. On his partner's side, the expansion is represented by the Three of Wands on top of the King of Swords, so he's not entirely opposed to Julian's idea. With the Two of Wands at the bottom, Julian's partner prefers to be more conservative in his approach. He wants to be certain they're not biting off more than they can chew. The Two of Pentacles is auspicious to him, so the management is also favorable to his idea.

Based on their position within the spread, even though by rank, Julian's partner (or his arguments) seems to have a greater weight, it is Julian who comes out on top, as he is represented in the first row. This suggests that he might be pushing a bit harder to do things his way.

Elemental aspects:

- There are four fire cards, one in each corner: The Three of Wands, the Knight of Wands, the Two of Wands and the Six of Wands.
- Three air cards: The King of Swords, The Magician and the Nine of Swords.

- One earth card: The Two of Pentacles.
- One water card: The Chariot.

Fire and air are the driving force. This is a situation that is moving fast and in which decisions need to be made quickly. Since fire overpowers air, and because it is not ill-aspected, this might be a situation in which the drive to act has greater weight than the rational considerations. We see this also with air, which is a little bit negatively aspected with the Nine of Swords. The spread begins with fire. It is interesting to note, from a numerological perspective, how the spread begins with a Three of Wands and it is doubled to a Six of Wands by the end, suggesting that greater expansion will bring greater success.

Let's give a look at the rows now. Three of Wands—The Chariot—Knight of Wands suggest that Julian and his partner have already gone through a period of observation and contemplation of the possibilities, and now they are ready to act. This is a confirmation that it is a good moment to proceed.

King of Swords—Two of Pentacles—The Magician indicates that Julian and his partner are equipped on an intellectual level, as well as a skill level, to deal with the expansion, even though it may require them to reorganize how they have been working so far.

Two of Wands—Nine of Swords—Six of Wands suggests that the fear and worry about making a mistake makes the more conservative option (keeping the second location nearby) a more desirable option. However, there is no substantiation for the worry shown by the Nine of Swords, suggesting that keeping the second location nearby is not a requirement for it to succeed.

In this case, I would like to check the columns, too, as well as knight a couple of cards to make sure that there is enough substantiation for this conclusion.

The first column, Three of Wands—King of Swords—Two of Wands, reiterates the conservative approach that one side prefers to take out of caution, after passing it through the filter of rationality.

The second column, The Chariot—Two of Pentacles—Nine of Swords, also reinforces the idea that there are interfering fears around the ability to keep up with both locations. At the same time, this row confirms that there is nothing to suggest that there is a tangible reason to sustain that fear. The third column, Knight of Wands—The Magician—Six of Pentacles, strengthens the argument that they are ready to tackle the challenge.

Let's take note of a few of the knighting positions. The King of Swords and the Knight of Wands knight one another. Despite having different opinions as to how to proceed, Julian and his partner are on the same team. The King of Swords knights the Six of Wands, suggesting that he believes in the success of the endeavor. On a different note, the other knighting of the Knight of Wands is by the Nine of Swords, suggesting that even though Julian is ready to act, he also has fears that he hasn't shared.

It is interesting as well to note that The Magician knights both the Three and the Two of Wands, which suggests that the partners are equipped to deal with either option.

So, let's return to the question:

"Would it be better for Julian's business to open a second location in a different city or closer by?"

Neither option would be bad, based on the cards. The two business partners seem to be determined to make it work, and, though they have diverse fears and opinions with one of them being more ready to take risks while the other would prefer a more conservative approach, the reality is that they are both committed to the best possible management of the business. They both seek to make the best possible decision.

Considering that they are well equipped to make either decision, the directness of the three main cards seems to favor the idea of choosing a more distant location for this expansion. So, if there is a need to commit to an answer, that would be it. However, they seem to be equipped to move forward following either plan and to do it successfully.

Conclusions

After practicing these two examples, you may have noticed that each reading required a different set of techniques. This illustrates how it is not always necessary to use every single interpretative option every time. Instead, use whatever is necessary based on the needs of your spread, question, and context, as well as based on the cards on the table.

In the first reading, it made sense to explore the knighting connections of the cards that seemed to "break" the flow of the reading. However, it was redundant with other cards.

In the case of the second reading, where there were two people involved and two Court Cards on the table, exploring the relational dynamics of those two cards becomes almost a requirement. On the other hand, with the exception of the quick note about the Three and Six of Wands, investigating the numerological aspects wasn't necessary.

The reading and the context will let you know what is needed each time. After a while, this will become second nature. You will pick up on the information described here without having to consciously think about it. You will only have to scan the reading to know which interpretative techniques to use.

If you are using a technique that isn't necessary, you will probably notice that it is giving you redundant information. This is, in a way, a good thing, because it offers you further substantiation for your interpretation, but it doesn't add more to it.

In the worst-case scenario, you may simply realize that you could have done the reading without applying a technique. No harm, no foul, and a lesson learned. Don't be afraid to experiment with your Nine Card Tableau and its techniques.

Chapter 9

The Map around the Querent

Another use for the Nine Card Tableau is as a map to locate the querent's position in the situation you're reading on. Using this method, you can create a strategy that helps the querent navigate the matter and circumvent potential obstacles. This way they may be able to avoid any "plot twists" in the road, or at least be forewarned about them.

The idea is to use the location of the querent's significator card and the cards surrounding it to create a path for the querent to travel. To do this, we must pay attention to where the significator falls, and what this position adds to the interpretation of the situation.

If the significator falls in one of the main positions, those that are considered the spine of the reading, then we have information about how much power the querent has over the circumstances.

When it lands in the nuance position, on the top left, it indicates that the querent's actions and attitude will influence the rest of the cards, and the rest of the development of the situation, since their vantage point will prompt certain actions that will have an impact. With this in mind, if the rest of the spread doesn't reveal promising developments, further questions may be in order to see how to lead to a more satisfactory outcome.

In the case that the significator lands in the core position, it is a sign that the querent is either well-grounded or very set in their intentions (unless surrounding cards directly contradict this) and that the querent is enjoying a really good perspective of the situation, which will impact any decisions that are made in the situation for the best. For us readers, this is an ideal position to read with because we can see what lies on the right and left, auspiciously and inauspiciously to the querent, as well as what is in their mind, with the card on top, and what they have direct influence over, with the card at the bottom.

Lastly, if the significator falls on the outcome position, it is a confirmation that the querent will have the final say over the way things go or that at least they have the power to change the situation. Surely, our actions always have an impact, but in this case, the querent is presented in a stronger position than other influences, with greater room to maneuver.

But what if it lands in any other position? Well, this tells us something about the querent, too.

When we find the querent's significator in the past row, it is a telling sign that the querent played a part in getting to the current situation. While they are not in a position to change the past, of course, this positioning highlights the importance of learning from the past and from their part in the situation. This realization can be key in sorting out the matter, or it may help them in any other way.

A significator found in the middle row, the one that speaks of the present or current developments, usually suggests that the querent found themselves in the situation not necessarily through their own doing. The advantage of this position is that they have room to make changes and impact future developments.

A significator found in the last row suggests that the querent's time to act will come later. The situation needs to develop a bit more before it is the right moment to act on it. In this kind of scenario, understanding the development of the situation and how it will unfold is helpful so that the querent is equipped to intervene in the right circumstances.

These different perspectives offer us hints to guide the querent in the situation. This is the starting point of the navigation, the beginning of the journey through the rest of the "map" that is the tableau.

There are four card positions in the tableau that reveal a lot about the querent's situation. They won't always be present, depending on the position in which your significator falls. In fact, the only position in the Nine Card Tableau that will show the full four is the core position. This technique is useful for other layouts, such as the 5x5 Tableau or the Major Arcana Tableau, which are larger spreads. However, you can still use this technique with the Nine Card Tableau. Even if the four positions do not apply to where your significator has landed, it's worth investigating the ones that do appear.

The card on top of the querent's head will tell us what is in their mind, what concerns them, what they are preoccupied by, or what weighs on them. Often, the querent doesn't control this aspect of the situation.

The card directly below the querent's card, or at their feet, is what they have a direct impact on, what they have under control, or whatever they are intentionally doing or acting upon.

The card on the left of the querent is what is inauspicious to them, or what works against them in a situation. It can also refer to something that they are ignoring.

The card on the right of the querent is what is auspicious or favorable to them, what will go right in the situation.

A different approach is, rather than left and right, to consider what is in front of the querent's card versus what is to their back. This is the method I use when I read. What is in front of the significator's face will be the auspicious placement. What is to their back will be the inauspicious placement. This is regardless of whether the card is on the left or right.

With that being said, it's useful to remember the left is generally inauspicious and right is generally auspicious for cards such as the King of Swords in the Rider Waite Smith, who is looking forward and is not inclined to any particular direction.

Finding a Way Forward: The Tableau Map

This visual technique offers a unique way to discover alternative solutions in complicated, obstacle-filled situations. It relies more on working with what is on the table rather than with hard-and-fast rules. You can either use a preselected significator that you've shuffled in or use one that appears organically in the reading.

"How to" questions can benefit a lot from this technique. For instance, our question might be something like, "How can Elizabeth navigate the transition from her current job to building her own business?" or "How can Jane get closer to Charles?"

The way-forward technique aims to connect the person with their goal. This is why shuffling in pre-chosen significators for people and situations can be helpful, although if you choose to let them show up organically instead, you may be surprised to see how frequently they show up on their own.

These are the things to look at:

- Line of sight: What is in front and to the back of the querent. We've already discussed auspicious/inauspicious placements, but it's interesting to explore them here.
- What's weighing on the querent: The card "on top" of the querent. This will tell us about their ideas, hopes, fears, or obstacles.
- The obvious path forward: What is directly below the significator. This will be one or two cards in the Nine Card Tableau, but up to four cards in the 5x5 Tableau.
- Alternative paths forward: When the obvious path forward is blocked or unavailable, we can look at other ways for the querent to achieve their goal. To do this, we'll use techniques like

bridging or knighting to make connections and discover if there is a card available that could support the querent's goal. The cards that are jumped over represent obstacles that need to be resolved. The diagonals can also be seen as opportunities to take an alternative route. If there are no cards that suggest options available to the querent, it can be useful to suggest an alternative question or alternative goal to explore.

Let's look at an example:
"How can Jane, a mother, get closer to her son Charles?"

The Queen of Cups is the significator for Jane, while the Page of Cups is the significator for her son Charles. These two cards appear as far apart as they can get from one another in the Nine Card Tableau, with the Queen of Cups in the first position of the first row, the nuance position, and the Page of Cups in the third position of the third row, the outcome position. There are two things to take into consideration, though. The first is the Queen of Cups in the nuance position. If Jane considers there to be a rapprochement, it probably exists only from her own perspective. Second, the Page of Cups is facing in her direction, but she's turned her back to him. This indicates that the distance between them exists because they are not well synchronized, but that it is not a wanted distance on either part. We know that Jane does not want the distance because she's asking how they can become closer, and with Charles we can see that he's open to their connection because the Page of Cups is facing the Queen of Cups. But they are not speaking the same language here.

It's interesting that Jane's significator appears on top and Charles's is at the bottom, in an echo of the hierarchical fashion proper of relationships between parents and children. It's also interesting to note that what she has below are two fire cards, and what he has on top are two air cards. The core of the situation is the Ace of Wands.

With Jane sitting on top of the Six of Wands and the Nine of Wands, and the central card being the Ace of Wands, I interpret Jane exerts great control over Charles. Charles, with the Five of Swords and Six of Swords above himself, feels that there is no room for his expression or point of view, or that he has to let go of the opportunity to make his case.

Now, how do Jane and Charles move forward?

A column of fire and a column of air are at odds. This isn't a situation that can be fixed by Jane exerting power over Charles, and most likely, in the current situation, Charles's arguments are not compelling to Jane, either. The central row, the cards in between them both, seems to hold the key.

I like that the Three of Pentacles is on the table. This is a card that reconciles people. The Three of Pentacles, being a card of collaboration, suggests that there needs to be a middle ground for this relationship to improve. The Eight of Cups is behind the back of the Queen of Cups, and it's also knighting the Page of Cups. This suggests that, even if they don't like it, they both need to know when to let go. But with the Ace of Wands in between them, Jane and Charles both need to learn how to more carefully choose their hills to die on. If they seek agreements instead of trying to impose their own wills on each other, they are more likely to gain closeness.

Finding ways to allow for Charles's self-expression will help the cause. The knighting between the Six of Wands, the Five of Swords, and The Page of Cups indicates that Charles understanding how certain decisions are benefiting him can help things along the way, too. This needs to be a *true* understanding, and not simply Jane telling Charles that things are for his own good. Offering him a win every now and then will also benefit the relationship.

The Tableau as a Map for Locations

This is a bit of a rudimentary method, but also a useful one when reading for a querent who is deciding between traveling to, moving to, or purchasing property in a number of different locations. This method uses the tableau itself as a map and offers insight into which location is best.

I once read for one of my regular querents who needed a quick reading on which business trips they should prioritize. Since the reading wasn't booked in advance, I didn't have the time to look into each individual location, so this is what I resolved instead.

The destinations that my querent had in mind were Dubai, the Cayman Islands, Bangladesh, and Switzerland, and their home location was in the southern United States. Thinking of the traditional presentation of a planisphere, with America on the left and Asia on the right, and considering that all of those locations were to the east of my querent's location, I pulled a Nine Card Tableau to represent that world map. I determined that the areas of the tableau with the most promising cards would be the trips that needed prioritizing.

This spread is shown on page 116.

I quickly discarded the Cayman Islands. They were the closest destination to the east of the querent and there were three unpromising cards in the left column. I concluded that it wouldn't be a prosperous trip and that it could be skipped.

Next up, I saw the Three of Cups right at the center of the spread. That central location, which is completely surrounded, made me think of Switzerland, and how that would probably be a pleasant trip, one that could be used for networking and socializing. However, it wasn't necessarily pressing.

Dubai and Bangladesh were the two locations left, and the ones that were the furthest east from the querent. In terms of longitude, Dubai is slightly north of Bangladesh, so I assigned The Wheel of Fortune to Bangladesh as the most promising location to travel to for business reasons, followed by Dubai with that Nine of Cups, Switzerland, and lastly the Cayman Islands if it was a necessary trip.

This is one way that you can use the tableau as versatile tool that you need for a particular purpose—in this case, determining the order of importance for a number of business trips. This also works if you need to use the tableau as the blueprint of a house, or if you are trying to determine the best area of a city to look for a new apartment. Simply determine how the tableau will represent the space and your or your querent's position relative to it, and you'll be ready to go.

Chapter 10

The 5x5 Tableau

The Twenty-Five Card Tableau or the 5x5 Tableau is, so to speak, the big sister of the Nine Card Tableau. It has almost thrice as many cards, so it can feel even more intimidating. However, once you're familiar with the Nine Card Tableau system, it won't be too difficult for you to get a good grasp on this spread.

The techniques you've seen previously are the same techniques we will use here, only expanded. The difference is that the 5x5 Tableau contains several possibilities for an internal Nine Card Tableau. You can use this if need be, especially when you identify a card that is representative of an area of particular interest and you want to investigate the circumstances around it.

But before we get to that, let's start at the beginning. Why do you even need a twenty-five card spread, and when do you use it?

I'm personally not a fan of using this spread willy-nilly. This isn't because of any ominous or superstitious reason. Nothing is going to happen if you choose to go with a twenty-five card spread instead of something else, but there is such a thing as too much information. There are situations that simply don't have that amount of information available, so if you pull twenty-five cards on a situation that has no substance, you're likely to end up confused. Keep in mind that twenty-five cards are roughly a third of the deck. Most individual questions don't need this number of cards to be answered.

I recommend using this spread for the following situations:

- Longer timelines. If you want a detailed outlook six months ahead on a situation, this 5x5 Tableau might be the way to go. (It's not your only choice for a longer timeline, though.) It's also a good option if you want to do a detailed month-ahead reading. You can assign roughly one week per row, with the last row representing preparation for the next month.

- A situation where there are several open fronts or intertwined matters. For instance, a situation in which a couple who own a failing business together are also undergoing a marital crisis.
- When there are several options or solutions to explore. As you progress through the reading, you can see what option or options unfold and the outcomes of each.
- When you want an in-depth view of the past, present, and future of a matter with greater detail than you would get with a Nine Card Tableau.

And these are the instances in which I do not recommend using this spread:

- Most simple relationship questions. Any relationship situation that is unclear is likely to be even more unclear after twenty-five cards. The exception is a relationship with a long story and significant enmeshment, or if other life areas are intertwined with the matter, as in the example above. Questions about someone's feelings, about the reason behind a behavior, or about a new or short-lived relationship aren't a good match for this tableau.
- Very concrete questions. This is a spread that thrives either with more open-ended situations or questions, or with complicated matters. "Will I get this job?" or "How can I improve my performance?" are questions for a Nine Card Tableau, not a 5x5.
- Questions with a short timeline. Immediate issues or issues that will be resolved in a short period of time are not a good match, as there will be more cards than information.

As a rule of thumb, if you are in doubt about what option is best to choose, go with the Nine Card Tableau. You can always pull a 5x5 Tableau afterwards if you feel that the reading could have given you more.

Twenty-Five Card Tableau Techniques

The method for pulling the cards is fairly simple. While I have a preferred order for laying the Nine Card Tableau, in the case of the 5x5 Tableau I advise simply pulling five rows of five cards, with or without a preselected significator according to the reader's preference.

In this spread, there is even more room for patterns to occur and for absences to become glaringly obvious. I recommend taking a moment to scan the spread to let it sink in before you begin your interpretation. Don't be overwhelmed by so many cards! (Though it's easier said than done.) This may be unpopular advice, but you don't need to read every single card. I'm sure you have read books with words that you hadn't heard before, and maybe you guessed some of these words' meanings based on the context in which they occurred. This will happen when reading tarot, too! There may have been other instances where you didn't know a word and you simply moved on because that particular word wasn't keeping you from understanding the rest of the paragraph. This, too, will happen with tarot.

That is okay! When reading tableau, you will sometimes find that a card adds a specific insight when you apply a technique, but doesn't have a lot to say by itself. Or you may find that a card belongs to a pattern, but it doesn't seem to add much, or that it disrupts another pattern, which is a message of its own.

My advice is that you allow this to happen and that you focus on the paragraph over the word, so to speak. Single cards have a relative importance, like a brush stroke on a canvas. There are strokes that compose the main figure of the painting, and there are strokes that compose the background. Not everything is the face of the Mona Lisa. The trees in the back, the water, and the sky are also in the composition. Some cards have the same role as the background in a work of art.

The 5x5 Timeline

The timeline of the 5x5 Tableau is even more flexible than the Nine Card Tableau. The classic timeline starts with a more distant past in the first row, moving to a more recent past in the second, situating the present in the third, immediate future in the fourth, and distant future in the fifth row. This kind of timeline works well in complex situations in which an ample understanding of the past is required. The layout is shown on page 122.

If such an elaboration of the past is not necessary, but having some idea of the foundation of the situation is still desirable, there is the alternative option of starting with the past in the first row, present in the second, and the immediate future in the third row, moving further ahead in the future in the fourth and then the fifth. This is perfect for readings in which the main focus is the development of the situation, or for a more predictive approach where having certain information about prior events is helpful.

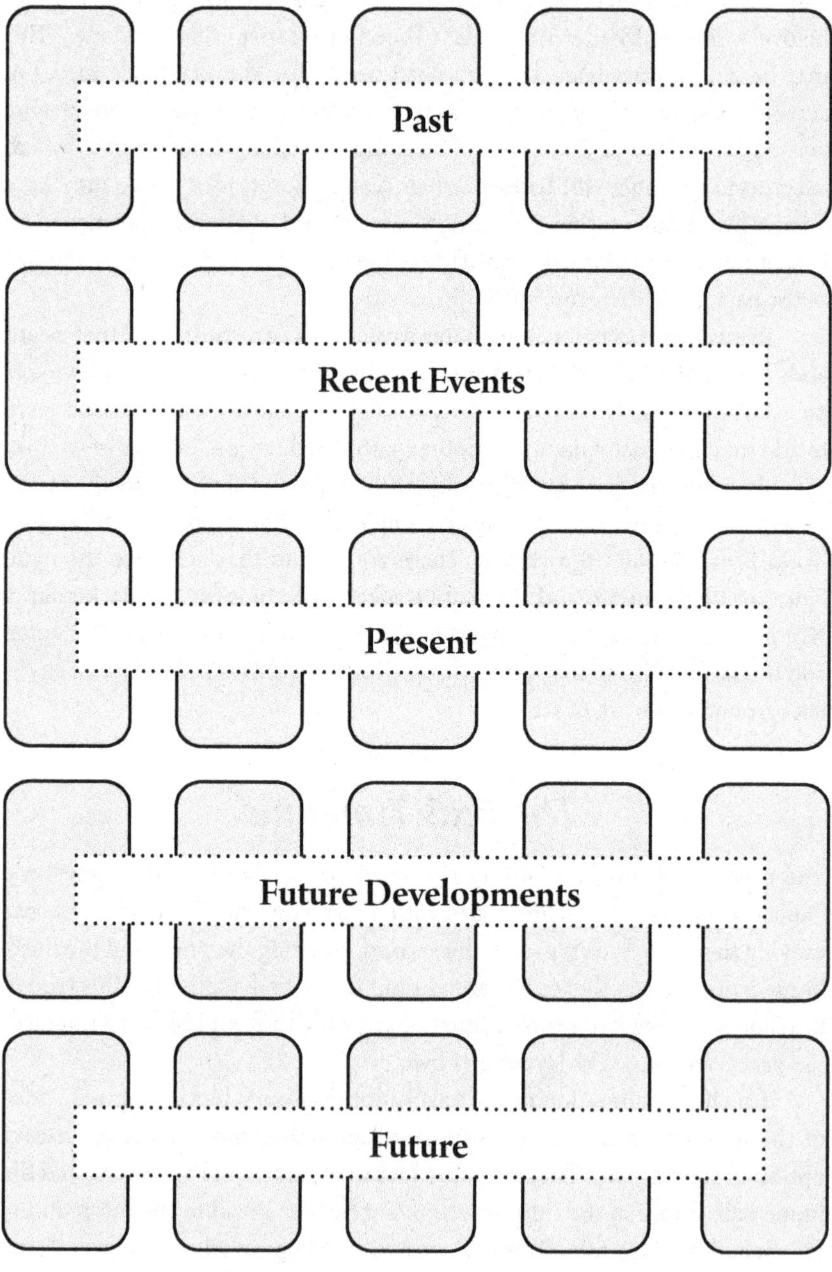

For purely predictive approaches, there is the option of starting with the present in the first row and moving further into the future as the rows progress. There is also there is the option to split each row into weeks or months when working with a predetermined timeline. There are so many possibilities, so feel free to explore and experiment!

The Spine of the 5x5 Tableau

The main diagonal or the spine of the 5x5 Tableau works similarly to the Nine Card Tableau. This time, though, instead of three cards in the diagonal, there are five. In the case of the 5x5 Tableau, the three main cards' roles still apply, with the card on the top left bringing nuance, the central card (the third card of the third row) being the core, and the bottom right card (the fifth card of the fifth row) being the strongest outcome card.

The two cards in between (the second card of the second row and the fourth card of the fourth row) are connectors of sorts. They can indicate how the nuance and the core connect, or how the nuance influences the core, or how the core connects to or influences the outcome.

Rows, Columns, Corners, and Bridging

Just like in the Nine Card Tableau, you can use rows, columns, corners, and bridging to deepen your understanding of the reading, only with more cards. In the case of the corners, you can choose to use just the external corners, or you can also use the cards that touch the core diagonally and apply the same principle to them. If you go with the second option, the influences closer to the core will have a greater weight than those on the outer corners, and, when looking at the bottom part of the diagonal, the core will have greater influence on the direct bottom diagonals than on the outer.

Bridging works the same as in the Nine Card Tableau, but considering that there are more cards, it may be extended. There may be two or even three cards in between two people cards that represent what unites or separates them, or in between a situation and its ideal outcome.

Rows are generally read narratively and used to mark the timeline. Columns offer supportive statements, additional information, or, if context so indicates, to reveal the next steps of a person card.

Knighting

While the practice of knighting works the same as in the Nine Card Tableau, it becomes just wild in the 5x5 Tableau.

To recap: Knighting imitates the movement of the knights in chess, linking together cards that might appear unconnected using an L motion. You can practice this motion by taking a knight chess piece or another small trinket and drawing it over the spread in a knighting motion until this becomes second nature to you. The number of possible knighting combinations is multiplied by the larger spread, and the central card, who had no knighting possibilities with the Nine Card Tableau, has now eight knighting possibilities, more than any other card in the 5x5 Tableau.

This is fascinating, for it offers great insight on the underbelly of the situation. Why is the core the core? How do the cards connect? Sometimes it can be overwhelming!

Many of the knighting combinations in the 5x5 Tableau will be redundant, serving more as substantiation than anything else, but others will be incredibly revealing. It is important to practice honing your knighting skills in the 5x5 Tableau. Over time, you will learn to identify when it is necessary and when it is redundant. Remember that you don't have to find something relevant every time you knight!

Additional Aspects

Considering that the 5x5 Tableau uses one third of the entire deck, having a bit of everything on the table is statistically to be expected. This is why patterns and absences become even more evident and relevant in the 5x5 Tableau.

It's unlikely that you will not have a single Major Arcana card in your spread. It's a bit less unlikely to have a spread with no Court Cards, although it would still be odd. It is downright impossible to have a spread without any Minor Arcana cards in a 5x5 Tableau reading, as the Major Arcana consists of only twenty-two cards. However, if your spread has less than half, or even less than a third, of Minor Arcana cards present, that would be a noticeable event. The same applies for the complete absence of a suit or element.

At the same time, it's more likely that you will have repeated numbers in a 5x5 Tableau reading, since there are more cards on the table, and less likely that there will be the complete absence of any one number. Keep these odds in mind when reading to assist you in your interpretation.

Tackling the Reading

Interpreting such a large spread with so many available techniques may feel like a lot when reading. While you don't need to follow a particular order, tackling the reading step by step is sure to make the process smoother.

Regardless of whether I'm using nine cards or twenty-five, I personally tend to scan the spine of the reading first. There may be times where at first glance your attention goes elsewhere. That is perfectly normal and there is no obligation to begin with the spine. With that said, it's a good way both to get a sense of the main energies at play in the spread and to start building a frame for the reading.

After the spine, I like to do a few additional scans of the reading. First, I do an elemental scan. Since an absence is much more pronounced in this kind of spread, if an element is not present or is present in a very low proportion compared to others, I take note. I also take note if I notice that one element is present in abundance.

The second scan I do is usually more focused on imagery and the body language of the cards, as well as groups of similarly colored cards and other pictorial patterns. I pay attention to any color that dominates the spread, or if there are any significant clusters of cards that share a particular feature. This could be a similar background, a common symbol, or a shared attitude of the characters portrayed in the cards.

Third, I look for numerical patterns and examine the numerical progression at different points of the timeline. By doing this, I can get an idea of what kind of flow can be expected. I tend to pay extra attention to middle-number clusters, since those are usually the ones that indicate troublesome times or challenges.

Once I've completed these scans, I look for Court Cards. If there is a significator intentionally shuffled in, I look for it. If there is not a pre-chosen significator shuffled in, as is usually the case in my own readings, I look for the first Court Card that appears and take that card to represent the querent. Once the significator is located, I like to check the cards present around it to get an idea of the querent's environment.

Now the time to begin meaning-based interpretation arrives, starting with the rows. If I encounter a card that seems to disrupt the flow of the reading, or a card that I don't quite "understand" at first glance, I knight it. Ten out of ten times, this card will make way more sense once you see what it knights. Considering the many knighting opportunities in the 5x5 Tableau, I usually knight only cards that don't immediately make sense, cards that are very disruptive, or if I find a card that is particularly relevant to the situation or that seems to sum up the situation. Don't get me wrong, you can knight to your heart's content, but too much knighting can make you lose the rhythm of the reading.

Let's explore how the 5x5 Tableau works in action. The layout is shown on page 128.

Amelia is experiencing conflict in her workplace. Her manager has taken credit for Amelia's work while she was being considered for a promotion, which she feels has affected her chances. It appears that her manager is undermining her, and she has raised the matter to HR. She wants to have insight into this situation, how it will develop, and what she can expect so she can be prepared.

For this spread, we have elected not to use preselected significators. The timeline of the reading begins in the present and moves forward into the future as the situation evolves.

Going with the step-by-step system, we begin with the spine of the reading. We have The Hermit in the nuance position, the Seven of Wands at the core, and The Wheel of Fortune as the outcome. At first glance, it's interesting that the reading begins with The Hermit and ends with The Wheel of Fortune, which is the next card in the Major Arcana. I can't help but tie this to the significant quantity of high number cards that are present in the reading. This suggests that these issues are heading towards a resolution, and it is possible that, timewise, the situation may not take too long to play out.

The Hermit in the nuance position adds a certain sense of isolation to the reading. The figure in the card stands on his own, and he is looking down and away, which gives the sensation that it's the querent against the world. It also suggests that Amelia may be a bit too focused on her own perception of events, and that she may be missing important input. The Seven of Wands right at the core speaks to Amelia's determination to hold her fort. She's ready to stand her ground and fight for what she believes in. The Knight of Cups connects The Hermit and the Seven of Wands, indicating that this is an important matter for Amelia, one that she is emotionally involved in, but also one she may be responding to in a way that is not necessarily helping her cause.

THE HERMIT.

JUSTICE.

THE EMPRESS.

QUEEN OF SWORDS.

QUEEN OF PENTACLES.

KNIGHT OF CUPS.

HIGH PRIESTESS.

THE WORLD.

THE MOON.

ACE OF CUPS.

KING OF CUPS.

TEMPERANCE.

QUEEN OF WANDS.

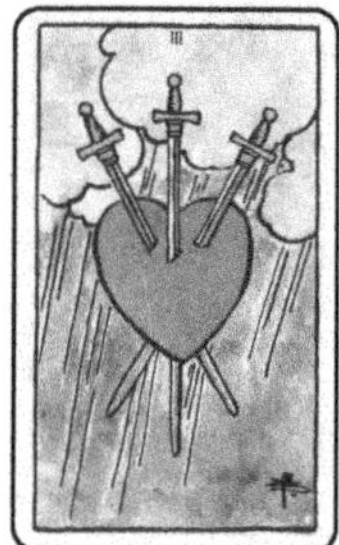

PAGE OF SWORDS.

THE DEVIL.

WHEEL OF FORTUNE.

The Wheel of Fortune in the outcome position is not showing its best side. The Devil immediately on its left suggests that there may be unexpected turns or that things will not evolve drastically. With the Two of Wands connecting the Seven of Wands and The Wheel of Fortune, we can deduce that this situation is likely to be resolved in a conservative fashion and will not require big changes.

The spine of the reading has given us a frame upon which we can build our deeper interpretation. The next step is to look at the elements present. In this case, the elements are fairly balanced in their presence. What we can see, though, is how the elemental distribution changes throughout the reading. Fire and water become very relevant in the three central rows, especially water, which is present only in these rows.

The combination of fire and water reinforces the idea of reactive and impulsive behaviors on Amelia's part happening as a response to the actions of third parties. We already noted that, numerologically, there is a significant number of higher-number cards, suggesting that the situation is close to reaching a conclusion. When looking for other patterns, we can see that every card except for The Devil depicts a single figure, reiterating the initial conclusion that this is an "every man for himself" situation.

As there is no significator intentionally shuffled in, I decided that the querent is represented by the first Court Card we encounter in the spread, in this case, the Queen of Swords. Amelia wants to make smart decisions, and she is determined not to let others walk all over her. With The World beneath her, she is ready to pursue this situation to its ultimate resolution. Justice and The Empress are to her back, on her inauspicious side, suggesting that HR is unlikely to reach a conclusion in her favor or, at least, that she cannot count on them as she would like. However, the Queen of Pentacles is on her auspicious side and both figures are looking at each other, indicating that she is likely to find support in this figure.

Who is this Queen of Pentacles? Based on this spread, I would say she represents a coworker. Both she and the querent are in a horizontal relationship, metaphorically on common ground, and seeing eye to eye. Considering that the Queen of Pentacles knights The High Priestess and the Eight of Swords, this person is Amelia's confidant and she is probably bound by the same limitations. This is a person that understands and empathizes with her struggle. The Eight of Cups below the Queen of Pentacles suggests that this is either someone who has an exit plan from their shared workplace, or that they might even be a former coworker.

Having determined that, let's move on to row-by-row interpretation. The first row presents the fight that the querent is undergoing. With The Hermit looking away from everything else, we understand this is a very isolating experience for Amelia. Justice and The Empress seem to represent HR and Amelia's problematic manager, respectively, while we have Amelia and the person who supports her in the opposite corner. Knighting Justice, we find connections between Justice and The Moon, Justice and the Seven of Wands, and Justice and The World. This suggests that HR doesn't have all the information or that the information that they have is distorted. It also suggests that they are seeking to bring closure to the matter as soon as possible. The Empress on top of The High Priestess suggests that Amelia's manager is withholding information. The Empress's closeness to the Queen of Swords and the fact that she's facing her, even though the Queen of Swords has her back turned to her, suggests that she is aware of Amelia's movements.

Moving on to the second row, there may be a gesture of goodwill towards Amelia's efforts with the Ten of Wands and the Knight of Cups. The Knight of Cups, even though it is a person card, doesn't personally strike me as representing a person, but rather as a gesture set in motion. This is mostly because of its positioning right below Justice, and the fact that it is knighting the Queen of Swords. This suggests the goal of shutting down the situation with The High Priestess and The World, hoping that tensions will be left behind with that Eight of Cups.

What does this gesture of goodwill consist of? Based on the knightings of the Knight of Cups, which connects with the Eight of Swords, the Queen of Wands, and Temperance, I would say that there will be a lukewarm attempt at recognizing Amelia's performance but in a way that doesn't really present any tangible value to her, nor does it help her move forward.

Continuing on to the third row, the proposed solution won't bring Amelia satisfaction, since it doesn't offer the clarity that she would like into each party's actions, as represented by The Moon. The Ace of Cups and the Seven of Wands going in opposite directions seems to suggest that being focused on this situation may cause Amelia to lose her focus. As a result, she might miss out on opportunities that are available to her. There are quite a few cards that knight the Ace of Cups, but the two most interesting are The Hermit and the Three of Wands. We can visualize the Hermit walking away from the Ace of Cups, reinforcing those potentially lost opportunities. The Three of Wands, meanwhile, reinforces the idea that there is indeed an opportunity to expand.

The Eight of Swords and the King of Cups also travel in opposite directions, with the King of Cups, the highest-ranking Court Card of the spread, moving away from the entrapment of the Swords. Amelia will most likely not want to go the extra mile again out of fear of a lack of recognition and a feeling of being trapped. This is likely to cost her an opportunity.

This is reinforced by the fourth column: The Queen of Swords, The World, the Eight of Swords, the Two of Wands, and The Devil. This row resembles a "cutting your nose to spite your face" move, in which, as a result of feeling cornered, Amelia takes a more conservative approach that ends up with her in greater chains.

The fourth row, with Temperance and the Nine of Swords, indicates that Amelia will have trouble letting go of what happened. The Queen of Wands is not very positively aspected with the Nine of Swords at her back on the inauspicious side. This suggests that fear and worry will be the motivating emotions behind her future decisions, causing her to be more cautious with her endeavors, as indicated with the Two of Wands. The Nine of Cups at the end of the row suggests that she will find some satisfaction and indulgence in this change of attitude, indicating that she may be thinking more about her own comfort than about career progress.

The fifth, last row opens with the Three of Wands and Seven of Pentacles. This can speak of long-awaited new opportunities at work finally opening up for Amelia. The Seven of Pentacles and Page of Swords can represent a "what's the point?" attitude towards applying for that new opportunity, leading to a self-imposed impediment represented by The Devil. This situation ends with The Wheel of Fortune as the outcome card, symbolizing the cycle of Amelia's feelings of isolation and entrapment restarting all over again.

In this situation, I feel it is important to pay attention to the interior diagonals that part from the Seven of Wands downwards. This is what Amelia has control over in her current situation. Yes, it seems that she won't get the satisfaction she is seeking, but taking her resentment and feelings of isolation too far can rob her from other possibilities later on. The immediate interior corners of the Seven of Wands are the Nine of Swords and the Two of Wands. Fear-based decisions may end up affecting her chances for bigger and better things, as we can see in the expanded corners, which are the Three of Wands and the Wheel of Fortune.

Returning to the question, it appears that she will receive a noncommittal answer from HR. Despite the unfairness of the situation, it also appears that the influence of her manager is limited when it comes to causing further trouble. It is Amelia's reaction to this ordeal that may end up creating more limitations than opportunities.

Looking at the likely development of the situation and its result, it could be interesting to consider laying a new spread with a more specific question. I would personally go with a Nine Card Tableau and I would suggest asking about the best way to deal with the situation to get a satisfactory outcome, or the best way for Amelia to move forward from this unsavory event and improve her circumstances.

In conclusion, the 5x5 Tableau offers the option to explore timelines, motives, patterns, and connection in more detailed and nuanced ways, which is valuable in circumstances that require it. However, there is one risk with this spread: information overload. This is no bueno, and can be counterproductive when the goal of a reading is to clarify a situation.

You always have the option to add more layers of interpretation, and it is easier to add information than to forget it! So, if you are in doubt about which spread best suits a question, use a Nine Card Tableau. Afterwards, if you need it, pull the 5x5 Tableau.

If you embrace the tableau method, you will eventually learn what works best for which situations or even just for yourself. Despite my personal experience that less is more, I have a student who can read a Nine Card Tableau perfectly fine, but who is simply *ah-mazing* with a 5x5 Tableau because that is her strong suit!

The key to mastering the 5x5 Tableau consists, as most things do, of patience, repetition, and observation. And yes, mistakes are part of the learning process, so don't be afraid to make them. If you're feeling overwhelmed, go back to the basics, split the spread into different areas, or divide the process of reading into different tasks, and you will conquer it!

Chapter 11

The Major Arcana Tableau

The Major Arcana Tableau is a twenty-two card spread consisting of three rows of seven cards each. The remaining card is placed at the end of the central row. In this chapter, I present you with two variations of the Major Arcana Tableau. The first variation uses the twenty-two cards of the Major Arcana, and the second uses twenty-two cards from the whole deck. The difference between this spread and the 5x5 Tableau resides mainly in the addition of houses to the spread.

Major Arcana Houses

What is a house in the context of tarot? To put it simply, a house is where a card would fall if the deck were laid out in the correct order.

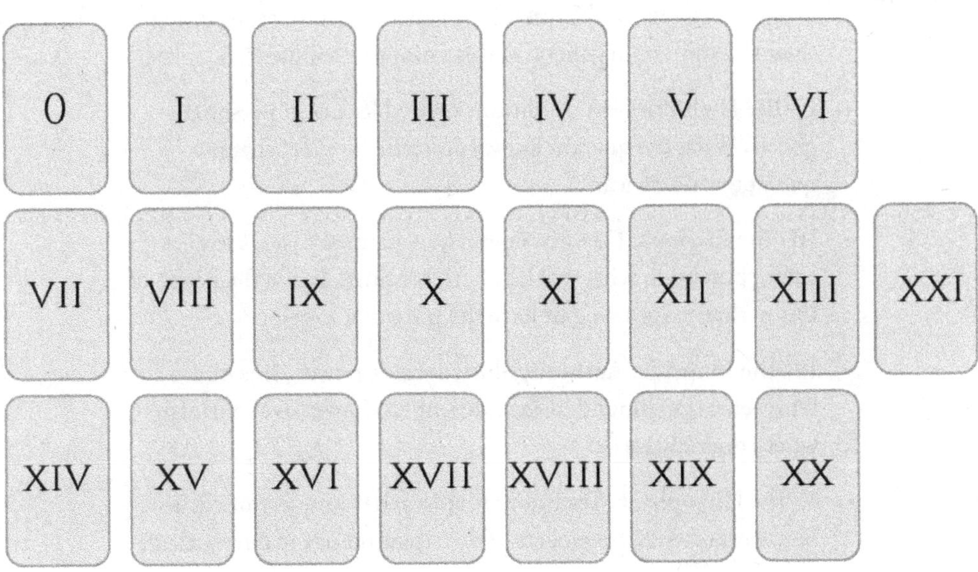

To understand how to use houses, think of a tin of Danish biscuits. Those tins have two layers of biscuits. The upper layer, the one that you see, is your spread, with the cards in whatever position they fall in. The layer underneath, the one that you cannot see, is your layer of houses. The first card on the left of the top row is in the house of The Fool. This means that The Fool gives an interpretative context to that card. The house of The Fool is a house of beginnings. If, for instance, there were a Five of Wands in that position, we could talk about new conflicts that are arising.

Using houses is a fantastic way to contextualize the cards when doing a general reading, or a reading where the querent has no specific question, but it also works with question or theme-based readings, in which each house will be contextualized to fit the purpose of the reading. In a career reading, for example, the house of The Lovers, which is the house of love and relationships, does not speak about a workplace affair (at least, not in most cases), but rather about relationships that are relevant to the context, or even about the vocational aspect of the querent's career. That is still love, contextualized.

Let's walk through the houses and their meanings:

- 0–The Fool: Beginnings; what is new in the querent's life; what is hatching; what new opportunities arise. This can also be the house that represents the client's area of recklessness.
- I–The Magician: Resources, skills. The card that falls on this house speaks about the querent's available resources regarding their situation or in general at this point in their life.
- II–The High Priestess: Intuition; self-led learning; personal gnosis. What the querent knows on some level or what the querent wants to learn.
- III–The Empress: Fertility, figuratively in most cases, literal in some; potential; what will hatch in due time. This is the house of things that are growing or have the potential to grow.
- IV–The Emperor: Authority, duty, agency, power. This house represents the things that the querent has power over, but also where their duties lie.
- V–The Hierophant: Tradition; that which is unquestioned. This house represents the aspects of the situation or the querent's life

that are accepted as is, not always in a positive way (though not always in a negative one, either). Influences that come from an upper hierarchy are also shown here.

- VI–The Lovers: Love and relationships. In a general reading, this is where we find the state of the querent's relationship or their love life. However, this can also represent other kinds of partnerships, as well as what has meaning for the querent.
- VII–The Chariot: Movement, travel. This is the house of progress, and it can speak of literal or figurative movement. This house can represent trips or moving to a new location, but it also represents obstacles that the querent will overcome or ones that are hindering their progress.
- VIII–Strength: Strength and resilience. This is the house that represents the querent's stronger points, what inner wells they may have to draw from to confront the current situation. It can also speak of what is becoming stronger for the querent.
- IX–The Hermit: The inner world; wisdom. This is the house of the querent's innermost thoughts and feelings, representing what is going on within them and what they are exploring on a deeper level within themselves.
- X–The Wheel of Fortune: Fortune, luck, and wealth. This house represents fluctuations, changes, the querent's fortune, or their financial situation.
- XI–Justice: Justice, legalities, bureaucracy. If there are any legal issues, they will be shown here. This is also a house that speaks of red tape and matters that resolve slowly. It can also speak of justice in circumstances that are not necessarily legal.
- XII–The Hanged Man: Stagnation; change of perspective. This house can represent either what is stagnant in the querent's life or what needs a change of perspective in order for the querent to move on again.
- XIII–Death: Death, endings, loss. This is the house that represents what is ending in the querent's life or what they are losing. This is also the house that represents what situations

or relationships will not return to what they were after the circumstances play out.

- XIV–Temperance: Patience, timing. This is the house that speaks of matters that are on hold, ones that are waiting for the right moment, or ones that are still developing. It can also be the house that represents what the querent is lukewarm about, situations or relationships in which they are not committed.
- XV–The Devil: Vice and attachments. This house represents what the querent is holding on to against their best interest, what keeps them tied to a situation, or what prevents them from seeing a way out. In certain circumstances, it can also be the house of sex.
- XVI–The Tower: Breakthrough, collapse. This is the house that speaks of either breakthroughs, what is falling apart in the querent's life, or what is most fragile in the current situation.
- XVII–The Star: Hope, direction. This house gives an indication of where to aim, or what the querent is hopeful about. In some cases, it can cross the line and represent the querent's self-deceit.
- XVIII–The Moon: Distortion. This is the house of what the querent isn't perceiving clearly. It can represent situations where they don't have all the information, or what they may not be understanding correctly, a perception that is distorted by their own filtering of information.
- XIX–The Sun: Happiness, joy. This is the house that represents the areas or methods through which the querent gets their way. It highlights what is working and what is going to develop positively for the querent.
- XX–Judgement: Consequences. This is the house that reflects the consequences of the querent's actions, for better or for worse.
- XXI–The World: Completion. The house of completion speaks about the aspects of the querent's life that are coming to an end, and what unlocks the next stage.

In this larger kind of tableau reading, houses are at play regardless of the chosen method. An easy way to determine the aspect of each card (if, like me, you are not using reversals) is to look at the interaction between the card and the house it lands in. See if both the card and the house support one another, if they seem to reinforce an idea, or if one of them seems to challenge it.

When a card lands in its own house, it reinforces the card's meaning and strengthens the house's dominion. Alternatively, it indicates that things will continue as expected in that aspect.

Using Houses in the Nine Card Tableau

While it is not at all necessary, there is always the option to add an additional layer of meaning to a Nine Card Tableau with Major Arcana Houses. For this, you will need to use two decks and two literal layers of cards.

Lay one Nine Card Tableau spread consisting of only Major Arcana cards. These cards will serve as your houses. Take your second deck and shuffle it, then lay another layer of cards, both Major and Minor Arcana, over your house layer. This second layer will serve as the answer to the question that is asked.

Major Arcana Method

The Major Arcana method is my preferred kind of tableau when I want a general overview of the querent's life. It allows me to see how everything is flowing for the querent and what the problematic areas are at a glance.

To benefit from this method, make sure you've "demystified" the Major Arcana for yourself, and that you're familiar with the card meanings. If you're struggling, try going through the core meanings questions list on page 16.

When using the Major Arcana method, there are a few cards that I look for in a reading to touch base on different life areas and to identify the position of the querent. This will determine their auspicious and inauspicious sides. The timeline is generally fluid, and the position of the querent relative to the spread can locate them in the context of the reading, with what is to their back speaking of past or recent situations that are still open, while what they are facing speaks of the future. Another timeline option, if you don't want to use this method, is to start in the first row with recent and current events, and move further into the future as you progress through the rows, with the last card in the central row being the last card that is read. This is the card that falls in the house of The World, completing the reading.

The Empress and The Emperor are significator cards. They represent the querent and the querent's partner, or most significant person to the querent in the reading. Their location and surroundings serve as a baseline to determine the querent's current location and what matters are most pressing. The house they fall into is of special importance for the reading.

The cards at the top and the bottom of a card that represents something relevant in the reading can tell us a lot. The card on top will indicate what is weighing upon that situation, and the card on the bottom represents the consequences. The corners act as influences. Knighting still applies as previously explained; if there is a card that doesn't make sense to you, try seeing what it knights and what knights it. The columns help sustain interpretations and add additional information.

The central card of the fourth column acts as the core of the matter. It is the house of The Wheel of Fortune, so either it speaks of what is currently "moving" in the life of the querent and thus what is a main concern, or alternatively its connection to fate and fortune brings attention to the card that falls in this house as a main theme in the querent's life, one that is relevant or key to the circumstances they are experiencing.

Chaining Houses

Chaining houses is a Major Arcana Tableau technique that can be very useful when further information is needed on a particular subject. To chain houses, first choose a card in the spread that you feel you want to know more about. Follow it from the position in which it's landed back to its original house. Let's do an example with the spread on page 140 that we will discuss a bit further ahead. Let's say that we want to know more about the querent's romantic relationship. We are going to locate where The Lovers card has fallen in the spread, and then follow it to the position of the card in whose house it has fallen. Let's try a practical example.

The Lovers is in the house of The Chariot, so we take note of that and find The Chariot in the spread. The Chariot is in the house of The Wheel of Fortune, so now we look for The Wheel of Fortune. Coincidentally, it's in the house of The Lovers, which closes the loop and leaves us with these three cards to gain additional insight on the relationship: The Lovers—The Chariot—The Wheel of Fortune.

Not every loop is going to be as short. In fact, it is possible that the loop will go through several houses, giving you a long story. I like to keep paper and pen nearby in order to keep track so that I can first get the sequence of houses, then interpret it. Note that chaining can be a very time-consuming technique and it's not always necessary. It's a "digging up" technique that I recommend using when other options are not giving you the insight or the level of depth that the situation requires.

As an exercise, try to interpret what these cards in these respective houses would mean when reading on a romantic relationship.

Clusters and Themes

The Major Arcana cards have an elemental component. In the Major Arcana Tableau, all the cards are present, so techniques such as the elemental ratio don't apply, but you can still look for clusters of elements. These are areas of the reading in which there is a group of cards belonging to the same element. For instance, in our upcoming sample reading, we can see that almost all the water cards are together. The Chariot and Death are in the middle row, with The Hanged Man, The Moon, and The High Priestess close by. This most likely highlights a particularly emotional area of the querent's present life.

You can examine other clusters, such as ones based on color, in which figures that show either a repetitive color or similar backgrounds fall together, or you can find cards that fall in a correlative order. While that is not always the case, I have found that on several occasions, Major Arcana in correlative order tend to point towards a period of time between the season indicated by the first and the season indicated by the last house of the cluster.

Let's explore a sample reading.

Lydia, the querent of this sample reading, recently moved to a different country to pursue a substantial career opportunity. She is in a long-term relationship that is now long distance, and she feels that work is too much. She wants a general reading to see what will happen within the next six months. The layout is shown on page 140.

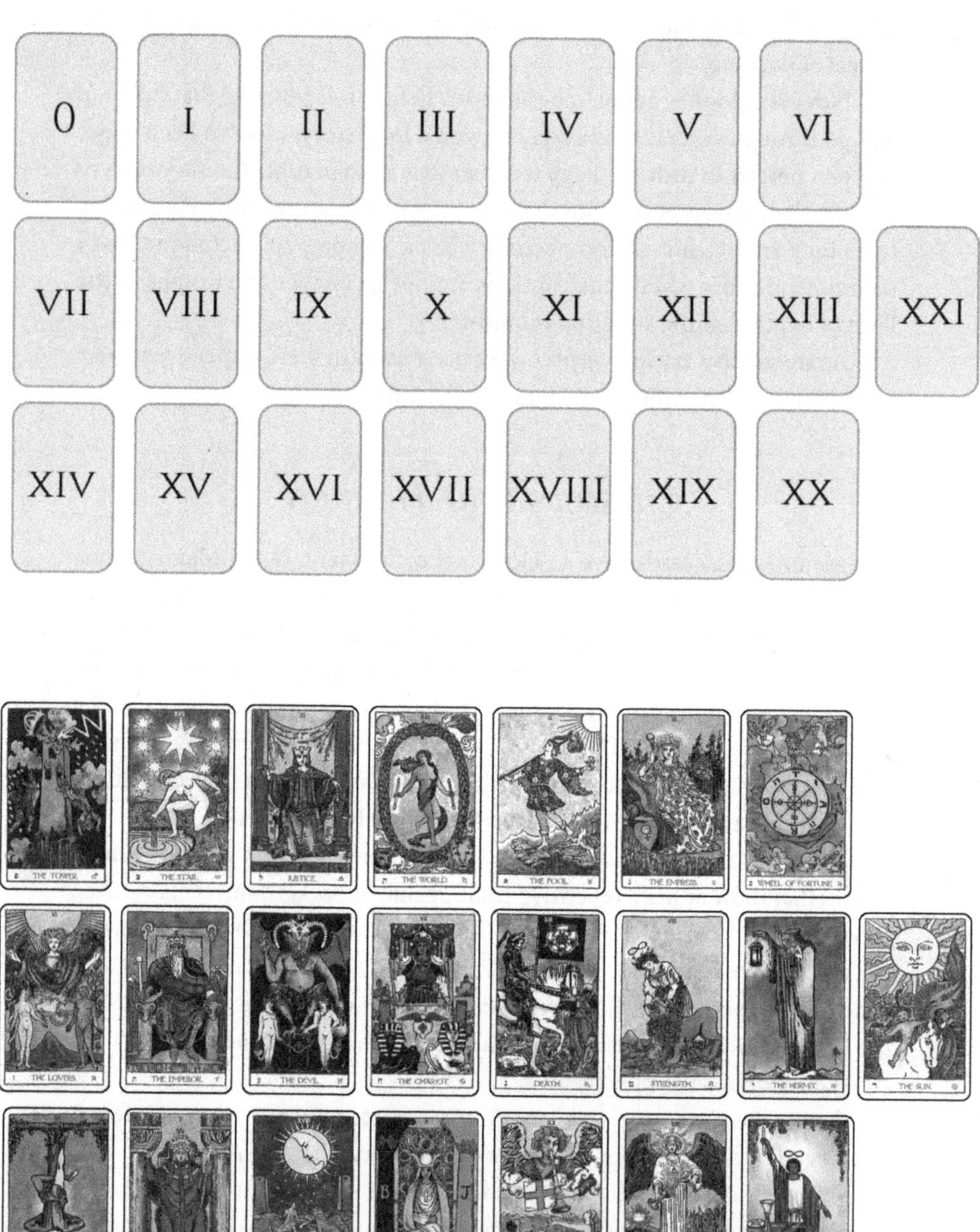
0
I
II
III
IV
V
VI
VII
VIII
IX
X
XI
XII
XIII
XXI
XIV
XV
XVI
XVII
XVIII
XIX
XX
THE TOWER
THE STAR
JUSTICE
THE WORLD
THE FOOL
THE EMPRESS
WHEEL OF FORTUNE
THE LOVERS
THE EMPEROR
THE DEVIL
THE CHARIOT
DEATH
STRENGTH
THE HERMIT
THE SUN
THE HANGED ONE
THE HIEROPHANT
THE MOON
HIGH PRIESTESS
JUDGEMENT
TEMPERANCE
THE MAGICIAN

The first thing that I notice is the position of The Empress, who is in the house of The Hierophant. I like that she's showing up in such a strong position, which indicates Lydia's potential to ground herself in her new location. The fact that she's showing up on the top row tells us that Lydia's pretty much in charge of the situation, even if she's finding it difficult. There's ample room for her to maneuver.

With The Fool in The Empress's inauspicious placement and in the house of The Emperor, we can confirm that this new beginning has not been easy for her. She doesn't feel in charge, even though her position is stronger than she may realize. The Wheel of Fortune in The Empress's auspicious placement in the house of The Lovers suggests that there will be favorable changes for her and that she will be able to connect on an emotional level with this new location, as well as connect with other people. She is right on top of Strength, which is in the house of The Hanged Man, suggesting that she has the necessary skills and perseverance to shift the situation in her favor.

Since we know that Lydia has a partner, the next step is to locate The Emperor. He is in the second row, in the house of Strength. It's worth noting that The Emperor and The Empress are facing away from each other, which indicates that they are not currently united. The Lovers is on the inauspicious side of The Emperor, in the house of The Chariot. This suggests that Lydia's partner sees the distance between them as a negative influence over the relationship, and that it makes the relationship complicated for him. The Devil in the house of The Hermit on his auspicious side suggests that he feels isolated. The Emperor standing right between The Lovers and The Devil can indicate that there's a certain dependency on the relationship on his side. The fact that it's in his auspicious side can be a sign that he has the power to change that, but he may be quite trapped in his current vision of things. With The Star on top of The Emperor, he's hoping to gain a sense of direction. The Hierophant below The Emperor, though, means he is probably comfortable maintaining the status quo and unlikely to make changes.

If we continue exploring the relationship by chaining houses, we can follow The Lovers to the Chariot and The Chariot to The Wheel of Fortune. This strengthens the idea of a tumultuous relationship as a result of the distance. The first column with The Tower—The Lovers—The Hanged Man also speaks of further trouble in the relationship, suggesting that the rupture of the established dynamics can lead to distance and stagnation in this bond, especially since The Hanged Man falls on the house of Temperance, which doubles down on passivity and can end up creating too much inaction.

The central, or "core" card, is The Chariot, which is interesting, considering the recent change of country. The Chariot in the house of The Wheel of Fortune seems to say that, despite it all, Lydia is where she needs to be, and this journey is part of her path. The World on top and The High Priestess at the bottom of The Chariot seem to reinforce the thought that a chapter of her life has ended, and now she's heading towards a place of greater independence and self-discovery. The knightings of The Chariot seem to be promising: The Star, The Empress, The Hierophant, and Temperance. Over time, Lydia will regain a sense of agency and direction that will allow her to grow and establish herself in her new location.

Let's read in a narrative way:

Looking at the first row, this beginning has been harsh. It has probably disrupted more things than Lydia anticipated. She's got the necessary skills to find a sense of direction in this new place, though the combination of The Tower and The Star screams "rude awakening" and confirms that she needs to continue to adjust her expectations. She's on her own when it comes to learning the ins and outs of this new place, since there may not be a lot of help available to navigate it.

The World in the house of The Empress affirms that she has left a chapter of her life behind for good, and that she's in the right position to grow. The Fool in the house of The Emperor brings the readiness for the challenge, even though she doesn't know how yet. She is growing roots and has seen only a small part of what is yet to come, as suggested with the unfolding of The Wheel of Fortune right in front of her. The Wheel of Fortune is in the house of The Lovers, which brings changes and instability to the relationship. We know this because The Lovers, in the house of The Chariot in the second row, surrounded by The Tower and The Hanged Man, shows a delicate situation in matters of the heart.

The second row with The Lovers, The Emperor, and The Devil indicates that the querent will need to take charge of the romantic situation and recognize the ways the current state of events is holding her back. The Devil in the house of The Hermit suggests that, at the time being, the relationship may be causing further isolation instead of being a source of support for Lydia. The Hermit in the house of Death at the end of the row seems to indicate a difficult change that involves further solitude. The Chariot, Death, and Strength in the house of The Hanged Man may indicate that Lydia and her partner will be taking a break to reconsider their situation and see if they are truly ready to make things work long-distance. The idea of taking a break in the relationship is also reinforced by The Hanged Man below The Lovers. This is pausing the collapse of The Tower over the relationship, indicating that there will be some space taken.

Aside from the relationship issues, Death in the house of Justice also knights Justice in the house of The High Priestess, which points to an end of any bureaucratic complications. This will facilitate things for Lydia in her new location.

Entering the last row, The Hanged Man in the house of Temperance suggests that Lydia will have to change her approach if she wants to make progress. Otherwise, she could be trapped by The Hierophant in the house of The Devil in a situation in which she feels that she has no agency. If she gets ready to confront the uncertainties associated with her new location, she will make a breakthrough that allows her to gain a sense of direction, as The Moon in the house of The Tower and The High Priestess in the house of The Star suggest. Judgement in the house of The Moon brings clarity. She will decide what she wants to keep in her life and what she is ready to leave behind.

I want more information about the changes that she will make and what areas these affect, so I chain the houses of Judgement, and it looks like this: Judgement—The Moon—The Star—The Magician. This combination of cards suggests that Lydia will focus on the development of her skills. She will embrace further uncertainty with an attitude of gaining a sense of self-direction. This, along with the limited interconnections of the relationship in the spread, makes me thing that it's likely that she'll move on from the relationship. Instead, that professional and developmental focus will take the front seat, with Temperance in between Judgement and The Magician. This will be a subtle transformation over time. The Magician in the house of Judgement is also an indicator that she will receive due praise for her skill, which will translate to a greater satisfaction in her profession.

With The Sun in the house of The World closing the spread, we might say that all's well that ends well! Wrapping up her previous life to fully embrace the opportunities that come in her new one will prove to be the right choice and one that brings her joy.

The Full-Deck Method

In the full-deck method, we'll lay a twenty-two card spread utilizing the entire deck, not just the Major Arcana. The full-deck method uses a combination of tableau techniques in combination with houses. (We will not be chaining houses, as it is not possible here.) This method offers greater detail, making it very interesting for situations that require further scrutiny.

Elemental, numerological, pictorial, and other patterns of presence and absence gain importance in this method, adding to the interpretation. The houses serve to add a layer of context to the reading.

Let's examine a sample reading to get a better grasp of how the full-deck method works.

Robert is in the early stages of a new relationship, but his ex has reached out to him and wants him to consider a reconciliation. Robert is unsure of how to proceed. He feels excited about the prospects of a new relationship, but he is also torn about his former one. He wants to know the best way forward.

Isn't Robert in a rut? One of the first things that pop right out of this reading is the presence of air, with eight of the cards on the table corresponding to that element, followed by an almost equal distribution of earth, water, and fire. This confirms that our querent is in his head about this situation and considering all possibilities. There are only two Court Cards in the spread: the Page of Swords and the Knight of Cups. Based on the context of the situation, I intuit that the Page of Swords is the message from his ex that, in its inauspicious placement, has affected how he, the Knight of Cups, is moving forward in his burgeoning relationship.

Curiously enough, neither of the ladies is present in the reading as a significator. The Two of Cups is in the house of The Lovers, surrounded by threes, and the Ten of Swords with The Devil underneath in the house of Judgement. The Knight of Cups, our querent, is in the house of The Devil, and the Ace of Cups he's facing is in the house of The Tower. The Hermit in the house of The World gives a strong indicator towards the ideal resolution. The Ace of Swords is right at the center of the reading, in the house of The Wheel of Fortune, with the Three of Wands opening, and The Devil at the end. All of it seems to point out that neither of these relationships is the ideal for Robert.

Let's look at this narratively. The reading starts with the Three of Wands, suggesting that Robert decided to look for a new relationship. The Five of Wands and the Five of Swords follow with The World nearby, speaking of a desire to bring closure to the turmoil surrounding his love life. The Six of Pentacles in the house of The Emperor, followed by the halving Three of Pentacles in the house of The Hierophant right before the Two of Cups, suggests that a conscious and practical choice was made to let this new person in. While it seemed like a good idea, this decision was not motivated by romantic feelings so much as by feelings of comfort. This is not a negative thing, but in this particular case it can point towards a desire to fill the void more than an honest desire for a new relationship. The Two of Cups knights Strength in the house of Death and the Two of Swords in the house of The Sun, which, to me, maintains that "forced" sensation.

In the central row, five out of seven cards are in the element of air, and the entire row represents the conflict that Robert feels choosing between these two options. The Three of Cups is in the house of The Hanged Man, leaving things in limbo between the three. The new relationship, represented by the Ten of Swords in the house of Death and The Devil following right below, seems to have been damaged by this possibility of a reconciliation. In the future, Robert will not be as focused on the new relationship as he once was because he will be distracted, as depicted by the Ace of Swords creating that division right at the core of the reading, with its placement right after The Fool.

The last row portrays how the message, represented by The Page of Swords, reaches the querent. He then goes from being focused on the single opportunity, represented by The Ace of Cups in the house of The Tower, to contemplating options with the Seven of Cups in the house of The Star. This suggests to me that there is a significant component of idealization that has been awakened by the prospect of potential reconciliation. Those options in the house of The Star point towards idealized prospects more than realistic ones. Judgement in the house of The Moon is a textbook combination of clouded judgement, and The Two of Swords in the house of The Sun dampens the new relationship that it knights, with The Devil in the house of Judgement suggesting that there is still a strong attachment to the ex-partner.

With The Hermit in the house of The World, we can conclude that Robert is very likely to leave this situation as a single man. But, with all this in mind, let's return to the question: What's the best way out?

There are several indicators that the new relationship, as comfortable and nice as it could be, is not based on love so much as it is based on a desire to find peace. However, having been so shaken by the appearance of his ex-partner, Robert must consider the open wounds he needs to tend to, as well as the very strong attachment between him and his ex. The best way forward seems to be introspection and time away from both relationships, so that he can work through his wounds before becoming ready for a new relationship.

Concluding Thoughts

Now you are equipped with multiple techniques for layered reading, along with different spreads that you can use, according to the needs of your querent. Remember that you always have time to expand with a larger reading or with a different question! There is a time and a place for the 5x5 Tableau or the Major Arcana Tableau, but bigger is not always better. When in doubt, less is more.

Practice is extremely important to truly master the tableau method. You won't truly grasp it until you have practiced many times. Try it following my directions and then try it on your own. See what works for you, what techniques you want to employ, and which don't do it for you. I am an adamant believer in not reversing when you can consider aspects instead, because it messes up directionality, but I have a student who is an excellent reader who loves a reversal in a tableau. Feel free to experiment and see what gives you the best results. If you are too anxious to try this with a real querent, try reading hypothetical questions and take the pressure off of "being right."

In the next part of the book, we are going to use the techniques and spreads that we've learned in different contexts, and I will give you some context-specific tips so you know what to look for, what different situations might look like, and how to apply the knowledge you've accumulated with precision.

Part III

READING IN DIFFERENT CONTEXTS

Context is an important part of what card reading entails. The questions we ask provide the framework for our interpretation, and that context is key when it comes to accurate reading. In this third and final part of the book, we'll focus on the subtle art of understanding and interpreting readings in connection to the original question asked, ensuring that we don't fall into the belief that the cards are speaking about another matter, or that certain questions cannot be asked.

We'll walk through how to approach different questions, including the dreaded "yes or no" questions, the "this or that?" questions, and even those questions that deal with matters that are generally frowned upon in cartomancy. We'll emphasize the importance of recognizing how the meaning of each card can be altered by the context of the reading, and learn how to adapt it depending on whether we're dealing with interpersonal relationships, career-based inquiries, office drama, health, finances, or spirituality, to name a few.

Additionally, we'll explore descriptive and timing questions, those that deal with the "when, how, and who," in order to equip you with techniques that will help you answer almost any question in whatever form it's asked. This will give you the confidence and the reassurance that you have all the tools in your tool belt ready to tackle your querents' real-life concerns.

It's possible that, on a personal level, you feel that there are certain subjects that you're not comfortable reading on. That is perfectly okay! The only thing that I would like you to take into consideration is that you don't need to have rules in your divinatory practice that are imposed on you by someone else, or ones that restrict you because the "tarot police" decided that you cannot do certain things. Tarot represents life and, as such, it contains the good, the bad, and the ugly in its seventy-eight cards, which makes it possible to divine on all those aspects.

Tarot is a tool not limited by morals. This is not to say that you shouldn't have any divinatory ethics, but rather that those ethics need to come from within you, rather than from what an individual or organization has decided. My advice, especially if you are a new reader, is that you explore first and decide later, that you feel free to try your own techniques to approach different questions, and that, even if only for the sake of testing your own skills and getting out of your comfort zone, you try to answer your querent's questions as they are and avoid the temptation to change them, at least initially. You'll be really surprised what you can do.

Chapter 12

It's All about the Question

Tarot reading can be made so much easier if we just stick to the question asked. This will help us as readers focus on deciphering the cards in relation to the specific question, whether it's an "if," a "how," or a "when," and whether it refers to a lover, a coworker, a job interview, or a purchase.

Questions come in many different formats, some of which facilitate the reading and others that make it a bit more complicated. In general, we can work with a vast majority of questions. They just need to be tackled differently.

The generally agreed-upon "ideal question" is one that is concrete, direct, and leaves enough room to consider possibilities. An example of this kind of question would be something like, if we lean to the predictive side, "What does my love life look like in the next six months?" If the reading is more analytical, we might ask something like, "What should I consider before deciding to change my vocational field?"

In reality, though, querents will probably ask things such as "Will my relationship with so-and-so work out?" or "Am I going to get the promotion?" or "Should I move to London or California?" And that's if we're lucky enough to get a full question, and not a "Whatever the cards tell you" or "Just a general reading will be fine." So, what do we do with those questions that are not textbook ideal?

There are some readers who believe that you shouldn't ask yes-or-no questions to tarot, that "should" questions are a no-go, and that you should avoid questions with more than one possible answer, like the classic "Will my relationship continue, or will I meet someone new?" I believe, though, that the reluctance some show to yes-or-no questions is rooted in the fear of committing to an answer and then having that answer be wrong (which, I'm not going to lie, is a possibility), or out of a sense of duty towards our querents and a desire not to dictate their lives.

Personally, I have found a way to reconcile with the possibility that my answer may be wrong. It happens. Sometimes you do everything right and your answer is still wrong. It is a risk that we take when dealing with something changeable and ethereal, such as the future. But when we force ourselves to be uncomfortable and commit to an answer, our skill grows, and we'll be right more often than we are wrong. We readers are not the only ones who predict for a living; so do economists, brokers, and meteorologists, for instance. They make their predictions based on a series of steps, on an observation of patterns. Sometimes the crisis doesn't come or the storm passes when it was supposed to linger. The same happens when it comes to reading tarot, and the reasons why are mysterious.

The second consideration, the one that has to do with querent care, is deeply tied to our personal ethics. My stance is that I consider my querents to be entitled to their concerns *as those concerns are*. While I will inform them of the actual potential of prediction and their own ability to make changes, part of being nonjudgmental and reinforcing their free will is recognizing that they are free to come and ask what they want to know, and that, if they have trusted me for that purpose, they are owed an answer.

Dealing with "Yes-or-No" Questions

Not every single question has a yes-or-no answer. Sometimes, the resolution of a situation depends on many factors, some of which may not be in the querent's hands. I would say, though, that a vast majority of questions have an inclination towards one side or the other. We can, of course, then add a nuance to our answer, but the priority is to *find* an answer.

For this, we need to simplify the reading, making it easy and to the point. Remember (and this statement will make some readers gasp in horror): You don't need to interpret every single card on the table as long as you know what you are doing. You can pull a Nine Card Tableau and look at the spine: Does it support your question? Does it go against it? There's your answer.

If that isn't clear, pay attention to the elements. Let's say you have a question about whether a relationship will progress. Most cards in the spread are air, and there's some fire, but the only water present is the Five of Cups. That's all you need to see to answer no. When doing a "yes or no" reading, keep it as straightforward as you can until you find your base answer. Once you have it, you can expand your reading if your querent needs more information or if there is any nuance that you would like to add.

"This or That" Questions

Picture this: One day a querent comes in and asks you whether they should move to London or California. While a concrete question is the most comfortable, that is not always feasible. There is not a card that says "London" and another one that says "California," but there can be indicators in the reading that point to the answer.

In the case of London and California, an abundance of gray/dull blue backgrounds can speak in favor of London and its weather, while bright yellow and bright blue cards could make a case for California. Coastal cards could make a case for California, while having a cluster with The Empress, The Hierophant, and the Four and the Ten of Pentacles would point towards the tradition and history of England with its long-established monarchy.

The same goes for a question like "Should I stay at my current job or find a new one?" You may find cards that suggest stability and expansion but not movement. These would favor staying in the current job. Cards of stagnation, meanwhile, would favor a change. Perhaps cards of movement and struggle would point towards not changing.

The key is to interpret the cards in the language and context of the question. The answer is always there as long as you look at the cards while remembering that they are framed by a context.

Timing Questions

The dreaded "when" questions can be an absolute headache. I agree, but querents want to know what querents want to know, and it's our job to provide them answers to the best of our ability. My personal timing system is not awfully precise. I work a lot with seasons, and in terms of "soon" and "not soon." Sometimes I can work with days, weeks, months, or years, but I am not the kind of diviner who is able to tell you that you will find your next job exactly on December 5th at 1 p.m. I work within my limitations, but my system has proven to be reasonably reliable.

Something to take into consideration: "When" questions can be too optimistic. I can ask, "When am I going to sell ten million dollars' worth of books?" The answer to that is probably never. (Feel free to prove me wrong! I think I could live with the shame!) This is why the first step with a "when" question is establishing an if. Once we can confirm the probability of something happening at all, we can then look into when it will happen.

I pay a lot of attention to the suits and elements when dealing with "when" questions. Swords and Wands are fast and active. There is an ongoing debate over which one represents days and which one weeks. In my book, Swords is the suit for days and Wands is the suit for weeks, but a compelling case can be made for either option, so pick what works for you. Cups and Pentacles are passive and slow, with Cups often referring to months and Pentacles to years.

Once again, context is key. If someone asks, "When am I going to get married?" when they don't currently have a partner and there are a lot of Swords in the reading, the answer is obviously not "within the week," but we can translate this into "soon." This answer is in relation to the context of that question and the querent's situation. Soon would require them to meet a suitable partner, have a whole relationship, and then get married. In that case, seeing Swords as a year is a fast and yet a reasonable timeline for this particular matter.

If, on the other hand, your querent asks, "When will I receive my parcel?" and there are a lot of Pentacles, years from now is not the answer, but we can conclude that the parcel is delayed. Perhaps it is stuck in customs, and it will arrive at the further end of the delivery estimate, or even after that.

Some questions are better answered in seasonal terms. Estimating time with seasons has proven to be quite effective for me. There is a debate when it comes to assigning a season to Swords and Wands, but, to me, Swords are autumn, Wands are summer, Cups are spring, and Pentacles are winter. Sometimes, the presence of Major Arcana is also helpful. A majority of Swords with The Hermit and Justice in the mix can suggest autumn is the season of our answer, more particularly between Virgo and Libra season, as based on the astrological associations of the Major Arcana.

It can happen, though, that the cards point to winter seasonally, maybe because there is a strong presence of Major Arcana cards that suggest that timeframe with the suits contributing too, but it's November 30th and our querent is asking when the business that they haven't started yet will take off and become a main source of income. In this case, "winter" is probably a correct answer, but "this winter" is not.

Other options that we have when considering timing are the presence of slow versus fast cards. An example of slow cards would be Justice, The Hierophant, The Hermit, the Four of Swords, or the Seven of Cups, to name a few. The Fool, The Magician, The Wheel of Fortune, The Chariot, the Eight of Wands, or the Ace of Swords can be considered fast cards. If the cards are fast and supportive, this suggests a quicker timeline than if they are slower or seem to pose an obstacle.

Lastly, patterns of repeating numbers or numbers that are relatively close to each other may provide us a timeline. A six and an eight may give us a timeframe of between six and eight weeks, as an example. Use the context of the reading to determine what the best timeframe is, and find substantiation within the cards to commit to an answer. The more you practice, the easier and the more natural it will become for you.

Descriptive Questions

"What does my next partner look like?" and "Where will we meet?" are questions that I am asked at least twice a week. It can be unnerving when you aren't used to reading in context, because you risk giving a super deep reading into the most intimate trauma of the querent's next partner when what they really want to know is if their next partner is going to be physically attractive.

When you have to answer descriptive questions, whether that question describes a situation, an individual's physique, or their inner world, you need to think in descriptive terms.

How does The Hermit physically describe a person? It could be someone with salt-and-pepper or gray hair, or someone with a beard. (There are only four bearded figures in the Rider Waite Smith: The Hermit, The Emperor, The Devil, and a man in the Ten of Pentacles, so that's a rare detail worth noting.) It could be someone remarkably tall, who maybe slouches a little bit. It could be someone who wears glasses or some other sort of visual aid, due to how close the Hermit is holding the lamp and the fact that he doesn't see in the glow, but rather illuminates others.

How does The Hermit describe a person psychologically? An introvert. A solitary person. A wise person. A person that offers valuable counsel. These are just a few options.

How does The Hermit describe an environment in which the querent intends to meet someone? A spiritual retreat. A place that is not usually meant for socializing and tends towards silence: a library, a waiting room.

Looking the cards in this way when pulling a tableau, you can look at the core card as the most recognizable or relevant characteristic of the person, while the nuance card will speak of something that everyone notices right away. It may be a bit more behavioral since it is a nuance. The outcome card can be considered a characteristic that is noticeable later on. You can adapt the rows to a physically descriptive reading by using the top row to describe the head, hair, and facial features. The middle row describes the features of the upper body, and the bottom row describes the features of the lower body. This is just an example. Remember that the tableau is very versatile and dynamic, and you can adapt it to your needs.

Let's explore an example of a Nine Card Tableau for a descriptive reading. The question is, "Where will I meet my next partner?"

The Six of Wands suggests a celebratory or commemorative kind of situation. The combination of Death and the Six of Cups suggests that it could be either the commemoration of something that has finished, such as a graduation of sorts, or a celebration of a significant life-stage change. This could be a wedding or a retirement party, something that marks the end of a stage or the beginning of a new one. Or it could be a reunion between former students or old friends, a situation in which one reunites with people they haven't seen in a while.

The King of Pentacles and King of Cups bring a calm and passive energy. If this is a celebration, it's not extremely loud or crowded, since the cards don't show a lot of people crammed together. The Three of Pentacles suggests that people from different ages or walks of life could be present, which reinforces the idea of a social event. The High Priestess, along with Strength, also supports the idea of a low-key event. The Two of Cups in the end might point to celebrating two people. Personally, I don't have enough cards to concretely say that it will be a wedding, but it could be an engagement party or an intimate celebration for a couple who previously eloped. It could refer to the celebration of the purchase of a new home, a new job, or something similar. Given the context, we can conclude that this new partner will come into the querent's life as through their social circle.

"Whatever" Questions

There are situations in which the querent doesn't have a particular concern. They simply want to know "whatever comes up" or they may want just a general reading.

Just because the querent doesn't ask a concrete question doesn't mean that you can't ask a question to give yourself some contextual framework. If they want "whatever comes up," you can ask what is the most relevant information that your querent needs to hear at this moment, or what guidance will benefit them. If what they want is a general reading, my advice is that you give yourself a timeline to work with, such as a past/present/future timeline, simply to provide yourself some contextual framework.

General readings require good previous work to be the most effective. Often there will be a theme for the reading. If there is not, I suggest that you begin to work around the core card. The core card will tell you what the main concern is, and from there, you can use above/below/auspicious/inauspicious placements to determine more. This will most likely give you a good sense of what is and isn't working in the querent's life, as well as their main issue, what weighs on them, and how they plan to act upon it. Use the diagonals to determine influences and voilà! You have a general reading. Bonus points if you pay attention to present and missing elements so that you can add extra depth to your reading.

Let's explore an example of a general reading using a Nine Card Tableau.

At first glance, we have a pretty noticeable earth column right in the middle. There are three water cards: the Four of Cups, The Hanged Man, and The Chariot. The first two are not very positively aspected. There is a subtle presence of air with the Two of Swords, and some fire with The Wheel of Fortune and the Ten of Wands.

Overall, the spread is stagnant, especially in its first row. The main concern of the querent has to do with their security, perhaps regarding their finances, or the solidity of their business or career. The Seven of Pentacles is at the center with the Five of Pentacles on top of it. This suggests a fear that their effort may not be enough to make ends meet. They have done everything in their power to get things moving, but right now they can only wait.

The Two of Swords is to the back of the figure in the Seven of Pentacles, in an inauspicious position. Most likely the querent will not receive news about the results of their efforts for a while, and that uncertainty is playing against them. With The Wheel of Fortune positioned before the face of the figure in an auspicious position, we can determine that the querent will be able to get out of their rut. This is confirmed by The Wheel of Fortune, which knights The Hanged Man and then The Chariot, switching from stagnation to movement. There is still a period of worry and significant effort ahead for the querent, represented by the Ten of Wands in the third row. Their effort will be worth it and, if they plan and distribute their resources wisely with that Knight of Pentacles, they will be able to move past their troubles.

It appears that this current concern is taking up most of the querent's bandwidth at the time, which can lead to them neglecting other aspects of their life. With water being particularly stagnant in the beginning of the spread, I would recommend that the querent pay some attention to their connections and relationships. Air is the least present element in the spread, which would lead me to suggest that the querent try to find ways to unplug from their concerning situation and make room for new input. New ideas will bring a sensation of refreshment into their lives, which will likely offer greater clarity than being surrounded exclusively by duty and concern.

Since the situation seems to change drastically from the beginning to the end of the spread, even though it's through great effort, we can speak of improvement, but the lack of fast cards in the spread indicates that the querent has a longish road ahead. They should be prepared for the situation to remain as is for a while, without expecting rapid change.

Having a repertoire of different approaches to deal with different types of questions can prevent confusion and make it easier for you as a reader. Before you pull the cards, determine how you will proceed and what you will look for in the spread to prevent second-guessing and increase your comfort.

Lastly, have fun practicing reading for different kinds of questions so that you can learn how you personally interact with the cards.

Chapter 13

Reading for Relationships

You may have heard that the majority of tarot consultations center around relationships. In my experience that it is true, followed very closely by career-related matters. With that in mind, equipping yourself with resources to deal with interpersonal-relationship questions is quite important, and even necessary if you plan on reading tarot for others.

What are relationships made of, speaking in the language of tarot, and how can we identify their issues in the tableau? The elemental aspects are an important key when it comes to deciphering the kind of relationship the querent is in and what dynamics are present.

In general relationships, regardless of their nature, each element plays a role:

- **Air:** Deals with communication, or the lack thereof, as well as with the clarity one has in the connection. It can indicate peace of mind or agitation, depending on how it is aspected, and it can also speak of how the person is regarded in their relationship.
- **Fire:** Deals with the chemistry between individuals, whether sexual or not. In romantic relationships, it deals with the sexual aspect, but in other relationships it has to do with camaraderie, how the people in the relationship are getting along, and the actions that sustain the relationship.
- **Water:** Deals with the emotional connection, whether romantic or platonic. There are some cards that tend to point more towards a kind of connection, but the context and aspects will always determine what is going on.
- **Earth:** Deals with the stability or security of the connection, as well as with the material and practical aspects of a relationship.

It is an indicator of the longevity of the connection and of the overall relevance of the long-term connection.

Ideally, a healthy and solid relationship of any sort would have all four elements represented, but the reality is often that there is something missing or that a single element is carrying the whole weight of the relationship.

An excess of air can indicate a relationship with a lot of arguments, or in which there is a lot of communication but little understanding. It can point towards a relationship that creates many worries. It can suggest that a relationship is mostly text-based and that there is little movement in reality, especially when there is no earth that grounds the relationship. In the worst cases, it speaks of a relationship that is more of a hope than a reality. A lack of air points towards a lack of communication, silent treatment, or the absence of intellectual compatibility or common interests.

An excess of fire in romantic relationships can point towards a very intense, chemistry-based relationship with mind-blowing sex that has little foundation outside of it, or the kind of relationship that is very explosive with a lot of blowouts and reconciliations. In relationships of a different nature, it can indicate that kind of explosiveness without the romance component, or that this is a relationship for the good times but nothing more. An absence of fire speaks to a lack of passion and chemistry, as well as boredom and the absence of a spark.

An excess of water speaks of a relationship in which love or an emotional attachment is the main sustenance of the relationship, but perhaps there are no other aspects holding the relationship together. The absence of water, though, speaks of a lack of feelings and emotional intimacy. In non-romantic relationships, an excess of water can indicate that this is a highly emotional relationship and not necessarily in the healthiest way, while an absence indicates no emotional connection or understanding.

An excess of earth can speak of a relationship that is purely for material or practical reasons. A well-established relationship with excessive earth has become dull, too practical, and too oriented in stability without prioritizing other aspects. It can be a relationship of interest, whether romantic or otherwise. The absence, though, indicates a relationship that lacks stability and long-term plans, or a relationship that is not seen as something to build upon, but rather as something temporary.

Tackling Relationship Questions

The previous chapter revealed that an approach tailored to the individual question can make a difference in the quality and ease of interpretation. Here, we will approach a few different questions and reveal the best way to tackle them to make the most out of the tableau.

Incoming Relationships

"Will I meet a new partner soon?" or "What is in store in my love life?" are fairly common questions about relationships that have not yet materialized. These questions work best with a predictive timeline that starts in the present and moves forward. It can be helpful to add a timeframe to the question.

There are two possibilities: Either there is someone new on the horizon or there isn't. If there is, you can use the descriptive techniques previously discussed to give additional information.

There is a possibility that new romantic interests will show up in the reading in the form of Court Cards. (Let me tell you something: Knights very rarely represent long-term prospects; they're usually temporary.) There may be indicators of a relationship in the form of the cards that are traditionally considered "relationship cards," or based on the interaction between other cards. You may alternatively see a period of inactivity, usually depicted by cards that are bland with regards to a relationship, or that portray people who are alone. In that kind of scenario, additional information can be given as to how to make the most out of a period of singleness. The reading can be amplified with a new question, perhaps by asking when that new person can be expected.

Let's look at three different spreads on the next three pages.

SPREAD A

VIII

PAGE OF CUPS.

ACE OF SWORDS.

VIII

0
THE FOOL.

II

QUEEN OF SWORDS.

KING OF SWORDS.

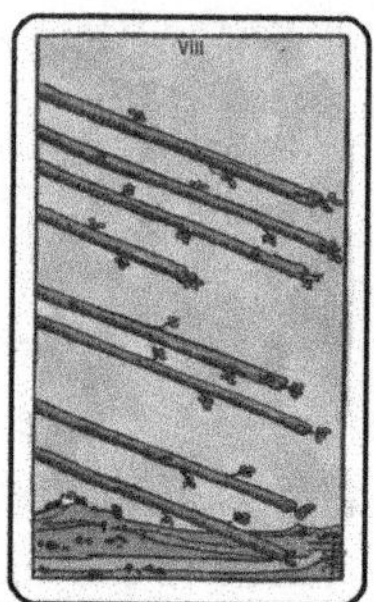

SPREAD B

SPREAD C

Spread A is an example of the layout that I would expect to see in a reading that heralds a new relationship. Spread B is an example of the kind of cards that would tell me that there will be movement in the querent's love life, but no lasting relationship. Spread C is an indicator of a period of singleness. Try interpreting these three spreads yourself to deepen your reading.

Existing Relationships

Reading for existing relationships is more about analyzing the composition of the relationship. What are its strengths and weaknesses? This is where we find questions such as:

- "Does this relationship have a future?"
- "Will we move past this rough patch?"
- "What does my relationship with so-and-so look like?"

In these scenarios, we want to look for signs of continuity in the relationship, and then for the quality of that continuity.

Some signs of continuity and growth are a healthy balance of all four elements that are positively aspected. At the very least, water and earth should be positively aspected and working together. Two significators showing up with a positive interaction is also a good indication. Cards that point towards development, growth, and fruitfulness in the relationship are ideal.

Sometimes, there is continuity present in the spread but no growth. This means that the relationship can continue in the foreseeable future, but that it will not change or develop in an essential way. There are dull or stagnant cards present, and the elemental distribution tends to have a presence of earth that is comfortable but not developing. You would see the Two or the Four of Pentacles, instead of the Three or the Eight, to give an example. This is paired with avoidant air, such as the Two or Four of Swords, and casual and noncommittal water, such as the Three, Four, or Seven of Cups.

There may be a high-numbered Cups card, such as the Nine of Cups, with nothing that adds further development to it. This indicates that the relationship is satisfactory for now, but not really evolving further. A Ten of Cups that either shows up at the beginning of the spread or is negatively aspected would indicate that the relationship has already reached its fullest potential. Fire is aspected in many ways in this kind of configuration. It is also frequent that you'll see a figure that represents the querent, but not their partner, or, if they are present, they are usually looking in different directions.

A "situationship" usually has a significant abundance of air and fire, but a lack of water and earth, highlighting the absence of an emotional and grounded connection. In this situation, it's likely you'll encounter passive, stagnant, and noncommittal cards.

In instances in which a breakup is shown, there will be cards that point either to an abrupt ending or to a progressive one. The elemental configuration will be dispersed at best or otherwise incompatible. If there are two figures in the spread, they usually appear in distant positions. The exception is instances in which the breakup is mutual and the relationship tends to have positive interaction with a common goal of separation.

Breakups and Reconciliations

There is a universal question everyone in the tarot world has heard: "Will we get back together?"

It's important that you are ready to tackle this one. My approach to these readings is that unless a reconciliation is clearly shown in the cards, it's a "no," or at least a "not officially."

I'm wary of the presence of generally "positive" cards in the middle of an otherwise dire spread. Remember: Do not let a single card carry the weight of an entire reading. Those cards may indicate that there will be a momentary rapprochement or affair, but unless there are cards that confirm commitment, I don't view them as representing a reconciliation.

Elementally, there are many distributions we can look at, depending on the particular situation. Usually, situations in which the reconciliation is less likely, or ones in which the breakup happened a long time ago, tend to present themselves with a mix of air and water. On-again, off-again situations tend to have a lot of air and fire. It's not terribly uncommon to find a configuration with a lot of water but either an absence of earth or ill-aspected earth. This speaks to instances in which there are feelings, but no compatibility, or in which the circumstances that surround the relationship are not conducive.

A sign that the initiator of the breakup is comfortable with the decision made would be a predominant presence of earth cards that speak of a practical decision. Seeing cards that don't prompt a change and are well established (such as Fours, The Hanged Man, The Nine or Ten of Pentacles) or those that confirm the end of a cycle or its abandonment (Death, The World, the Eight of Cups, the Six of Swords) also tends to confirm that the breakup is most likely definitive.

Let's see an example. John wants to know if he and Marianne will get back together. These are the cards.

The elemental distribution of the spread is composed of the following:

- **Fire:** The Queen of Wands and Judgement
- **Water:** The Moon, the Nine of Cups, the Eight of Cups, and The Hanged Man
- **Air:** The Star and the Six of Swords
- **Earth:** The Five of Pentacles

The cards suggest that not everything is said and done. The situation is yet to reach its death throes, but further developments don't seem to point to a reconciliation. The Queen of Wands as the nuance card seems to give Marianne the power in the situation. It suggests that things are likely to be done her way, or prompted on her side. The Moon and Judgement speak of uncertainty about the decision made, and Judgement points to an attempt at reviving the situation. However, this will be temporary.

The Nine of Cups and The Star suggest a moment of satisfaction that generates certain expectations, but the Eight of Cups shows how the fullness of the Nine decreases. A distance is created again, as shown by the Six of Swords and The Hanged Man indicating no further movement.

To confirm this, we can see how Judgement knights the Nine of Cups and The Five of Pentacles, indicating that this "resurrection" has no stable ground beneath it. The Queen of Wands knights the Eight of Cups and the Five of Pentacles, confirming that she should realize that the relationship has no stability and leave again. The Moon knights the Six of Swords and The Hanged Man, suggesting that the uncertainty of The Moon will turn into the future certainty that the right decision was made.

This is a fantastic example of how a tableau featuring the Nine of Cups and The Star, both generally considered positive cards, is not necessarily a herald of good news, or at least, not permanent improvements.

Feelings Questions

The age-old "How does so-and-so feel about me?" question is another one that you need to have tools to contextualize.

It's extremely important that you not lose sight of the context in such questions, which is feelings. The querent wants to know how so-and-so feels about *them*. Not about work, not about family, and not about the funeral of their great aunt, God rest her soul.

As always, check the elements first to see if there is an intellectual, emotional, sexual, or grounding connection. (In the best-case scenario, there will hopefully be a bit of them all!) Note what is missing. Is everything there but water? Maybe so-and-so is very comfortable and having a great time, but they don't have butterflies. Everything is there except for earth? They may not be sure whether they want this to develop into a long-term thing, at least not yet. No air? There may be a lack of intellectual stimulation. No fire? The chemistry is off, or the intimacy may be lacking.

Contextualize the feelings the cards represent by using the surrounding cards. For instance, the Eight of Pentacles together with the Four of Wands might indicate that so-and-so wants to work on building something together. They are curious and willing to make that happen. Ask the cards what circumstances are making this relationship difficult. You may want to look at the Eight of Pentacles and the Ten of Wands and think of a work overload, but in that case, the context supports a different interpretation. Rather than being burdened by work, this combination might indicate that so-and-so feels that the connection is a bit burdensome and repetitive. Bring the meaning back to feelings.

If there are figures, pay attention to the direction in which they are looking. If they are looking towards the right, it's possible, taking into consideration the surrounding cards, that they are hoping for a future together. If they are looking towards the left, they may long for the beginning of the relationship, or they may have their heart set in the past.

As we have learned in this chapter, the question has a direct effect on how we tackle the reading. I encourage you to take time to understand the question before jumping into interpretation, and to approach the cards accordingly with the situational context. Don't underestimate this step! Just as a doctor takes time to understand a patient's symptoms before prescribing treatment, it's a reader's prerogative to adjust our approach to the circumstances as best as we can. Spending a few moments to investigate this can dramatically increase the relevance of your reading.

Chapter 14

Reading for Career and Finances

In this chapter we tackle the second most universal concern: how we are going to pay the bills. Readings for career and finance questions are a very extensive topic, but here are some pointers to give comprehensive career readings in different contexts.

Just like with relationship readings, it's important to examine the presence the elements in these contexts, since they can often be a foundation for our reading.

- **Air:** Air relates to planning and strategy. It can refer to academics, whether it be the querent's academic track record or the kind of academic training desired by the workplace. It can refer to communication skills, the querent's five-year plan, or to intellectual stimulation or stress. For business owners, air can refer to data collection, information, communication, and ideas. Financially speaking, air has to do with financial literacy and ideas, but also with intangibles.
- **Fire:** Fire in career often has to do with the actual work, but also with motivation, the lack of thereof, or even burnout. For an entrepreneur, this can refer to the never-ending one-man show, always on the go, or it can refer to the actual affluence of the business and the movement that it requires, as well as its expansion. Financially, fire relates to what is active, so it refers to plans that are currently in action, money that is currently moving, and sources for money to come. It can also indicate where we are impulsive about money, or fast decisions made about money.

- **Water:** Water represents the vocational aspect of career. Here, we deal with meaning and personal fulfillment, making a difference in the world or having the desire to do so. For entrepreneurs, this can often be present in excess, indicating a sentimentalism or idealism that gets in the way of getting things done. It has to do with the social connections, networking, and even marketing. Financially, water speaks about fluency, about the meaning of money and our feelings around it, including our emotional reactions.
- **Earth:** Earth brings stability and growth. It speaks about the long term and about the solidity, or alternatively the stagnation, of the querent's career. It has to do with the benefits, as well as with how well-regarded or integrated we are in our workplace. Earth deals in reputation, seniority, and legacy. For entrepreneurs, this speaks about resources, raw materials, the solidity of the business, and accounting. Financially, it refers to cash flow, investments, inheritance, and long-term plans.

Questions about Finding a Job

Finding a job is a process of many phases. First you need to apply. Then, if you're lucky, you're called for an interview, and then maybe for a bunch more. If you're luckier still, you will be made an offer, hopefully a decent one.

How does this translate to tarot? With questions about obtaining a job, I tend to look for a lot for Aces and Pages. I frequently encounter Aces as leads or blossoming opportunities, and Pages as a sign that the querent will hear about an interview. If the querent is already in the interview phase, then an abundance of Court Cards tends to suggest that there will be strong competition. To see if my querent will get the job, I love to see a Court Card that ascends in rank towards the end of the reading. This could be a Knight of Wands that turns to a Queen in the last row of the reading, which suggests that the querent moves upwards with the process. Paying attention to power dynamics is very insightful.

I like to see cards that look settled and definitive towards the end of the spread. Ideally, I would see something that suggests stability. For example, if I see a Three of Wands closing the reading, I can conclude that there will be movement, but no contract for now. This can elicit the next question: "How can I find a job?" Or better yet: "What kind of job should I look for?"

Reading for Purpose Questions

"Purpose questions" refer to the kind of questions that have to do with what kind of job to pursue or what kind of change to make. This works just like the descriptive reading techniques we previously covered in our relationship readings, but with a career context.

When working with this kind of question, our goal is to describe the ideal career or job for the querent. I don't know about you, but I don't know every possible occupation a person can have, especially nowadays when new occupations and careers pop up so fast! But by describing the characteristics of a career, we can give valuable pointers or present ideas of the kind of career they would thrive in so that they have a foundation upon which they can build something viable.

The best way to illustrate this kind of reading is with an example. The question is: "What job am I best suited for?"

The layout is shown on page 178.

At first glance, there is a noticeable dominance of earth and water, so the job needs to be meaningful as well as stable. The Six of Pentacles at the core suggests that an ideal position would be one in which the querent feels that they are giving back. The Five of Swords as the nuance card seems to indicate a certain inner turmoil. Considering the querent's need for meaning, I would say that this needs to be a job in which they feel they are actively participating in changing the things they feel conflicted about. The Knight of Cups suggests that having an emotional motivation is important.

The Five of Swords knights The Hermit and the Three of Pentacles, suggesting that the querent may have some issues working in a team. They may struggle with the way things are done in a team environment compared to the way they would do things solo. This would be a profession in which, ideally, there would be common regulations and a network that supports the querent, but their individual opinion or approach would also be respected.

This description suggests to me that some sort of social work would probably be a good fit for the querent. Alternatively, a good profession for the querent would be one based on helping resolve what the querent perceives as an injustice, or an occupation that has a strong ethical component, but that at the same time provides a certain stability and predictability in terms of finances.

Reading for Career Changes

Questions related to job changes are a frequent occurrence. While, as always, the specifics of the situation will provide guidance that is relevant to the querent, there are certain tendencies that I have noted in readings about job changes when it comes to common situations.

When there are opportunities for growth within the querent's existing job, there is usually positive progression of Pentacles or Cups, more often Pentacles. Another positive sign would be water and air having positive interactions, indicating a fertility in the terrain and the potential for growth. A fast-approaching promotion is usually indicated by fast, fiery cards with Aces.

There is a variation of this. The promise of a promotion that never comes often shows up with Aces as well, but very slow or outright stagnant cards surround it. This indicates that, while higher-ups are dangling the carrot, they do not plan on actually following through. There is a sunken-cost fallacy that often presents, too, where the querent has already made a huge effort and quitting seems like a waste. You may see this with some combination of the Ten of Wands, The Devil, and the Eight of Swords, or similar cards.

When the querent is inquiring about the possibility of moving to a different company, I like to notice if it is the querent who initiates the change, or if it is the company calling the shots. My "querent leaves on their terms" cards are The Chariot, the Six of Wands, and the Eight of Cups, provided that the rest of the spread supports this interpretation. As traditional and uncreative as it might seem, my cards for a querent being made redundant are The Tower, Death, and the Five of Pentacles. I have seen Judgement show up with those cards when the querent's position is not in the first line of fire but where their position is still at risk in the future.

The Tower and the Three of Pentacles have shown up for me a few times as an indication of departmental restructuring, with various levels of risk for the querent's position determined by the surrounding cards.

Reading for Business Strategy

Sometimes, querents don't want to know whether their business is going to take off or if they need to close the shop. Sometimes they want to know the best strategy to stay open in troubled times, or the best way for them to grow their business.

In this situation, the elements become specific resources that are relevant for business owners.

- Air becomes data, communication, copywriting, the online resources one has, the client list, and the information that's necessary to run the business.
- Fire becomes manpower, charisma, selling skill, and the services or items provided by said business.
- Water is marketing, the emotional and social connection, the fan base, the followers, and the overall impact that the business has in society.
- Earth represents the physical resources, the cash flow, the sales, the properties that belong to the business, or the logistics and infrastructure.

It is important to adapt not only the elemental aspects to suit the querent's specific needs, but also the cards themselves. This will look slightly different for a business owner than it will for an employee. For instance, The Hierophant represents the hierarchy to which each individual answers. This can represent the C-suite for an employee, whereas it may represent the IRS for a business owner. Keep those changes in mind when reading for an employee versus an entrepreneur.

When in doubt, my advice is that you ask for more information. This is a way to perform the best reading, so that the cards can be interpreted with precision.

Here is an example. The question is: "What's the best strategy to launch my digital product?"

Fire is a prevalent element in the spread, with five out of nine cards belonging to that element. This suggests a quick launch. This is not the kind of launch or offer that goes on endlessly. This type of launch requires a limited-time approach that creates a conflict for the potential customer so that they must act now. This is indicated by the last row with the Two of Wands, Eight of Swords and Five of Wands.

The Four of Cups is the nuance card, but the rest of the cards on the table don't seem to favor it. Seeing that, I would ask the querent if they're thinking about offering multiple products. If the querent confirmed yes, I would say that the original strategy is not a good idea. This is substantiated by the fact that the Four of Cups knights the Nine of Wands and the Eight of Swords. These cards don't indicate movement and in fact suggest more of a resistance.

The Page of Wands right at the center of the spread presents a much more favorable way to go. The launch would benefit from offering only one product that has some benefit included, but that is also a limited-time offer. We can see this strategy provides growth and movement by looking at the Nine of Pentacles and Seven of Wands. The Five of Wands knighting the Nine of Pentacles and The Empress can be interpreted as a favorable outcome because of the question at hand, which is "What is the best way?" and because creating that disruption and movement is tied to growth and prosperity.

Life Advice for Intuitive Reading

As a final note when it comes to career readings, here's some practical advice that can improve your readings. You can interpret only what you have knowledge about, and when it comes to professional and academic paths there is so much that we are ignorant towards. Take time to expand your knowledge of different fields, get acquainted with entrepreneurship concepts, and try to think about them in the context of tarot.

You may have gone your entire life without needing to know what a hostile takeover is, but that may not be the case for your querent. Having some basic knowledge of different situations will add to your "inner hard drive" and enhance your ability to read on different situations.

This advice doesn't apply just to career-related matters. Learn about life experiences that are outside your wheelhouse, just as you learn about the ins and outs of tarot. Merging both practical knowledge and tarot knowledge is the recipe for magical readings!

Chapter 15

Reading for Health and Well-Being

The subject of health and well-being readings (as well as those related to end of life) is very controversial and delicate, and requires handling with the utmost care. This is one of those matters that readers feel passionately about, regardless of their stance on whether or not such readings should be done and in what circumstances. My own perspective has evolved throughout the years, and what began as an absolute no-no ended up being the kind of consultation that I accept in the right circumstances.

Being a tarot reader has humbled me in unexpected ways and has kicked me off my high horse on multiple occasions. Matters of health and death have been key to this transformation. I am, of course, not campaigning for tarot reading or any other divination method as a replacement for actual medical advice provided by a trained physician. That is absolutely the way to go when it comes to health matters.

As a citizen of a country with universal healthcare, I couldn't wrap my head around why on God's green earth anyone would ask tarot what they could answer with greater precision at their doctor's office. It took me a while to understand that walking into the doctor's office without a care for the cost of consultation is not the default for everyone. This realization made me more open to considering certain health-related inquiries. I am not qualified to give diagnostics or to propose treatments, and my advice for serious health concerns is always to refer the client to a medical professional. However, in my experience the vast majority of querents who have consulted me on a health-related question have begun by saying, "I know you're not a doctor."

I work with the understanding that my querents know the difference between a tarot reader and a doctor. I realize that often they either are seeking some sort of thread to pull to try and obtain answers because they have hit a wall when it comes to finding answers by traditional means, or they are seeking emotional and practical ways to cope with an existing diagnosis, separate from any prescribed treatment they are following.

For those reasons, I take a case-by-case approach to health and well-being readings. I consider the things that I feel I can ethically work with, as well as whether the person I'm reading for has an accurate idea of what I can provide in this aspect. Your mileage may vary, of course. Ultimately, you are the best judge of what you are comfortable with in your practice, and where your boundaries lie.

In matters of health and well-being, the elemental aspects can be viewed either as part of our body or as different levels to our health.

- Air deals with mental health as a key layer to our well-being. Physically speaking, it has to do with our nervous system, which transmits information through our bodies, and the respiratory system. It also deals with rest and sleep.
- Fire deals with our levels of activity and with our most basic needs. It relates to our organs, which keep our bodies functioning, as well as with our levels of energy and stamina. It is connected to our reproductive system.
- Water deals with our emotional health. It relates to the fluids in our bodies: blood, lymph, gastric fluids, sexual fluids, urine, and so on. It has a connection with the circulatory and excretory systems.
- Earth deals with physical health. It relates to our locomotive system: our muscles, bones, joints, skin. What carries us around, in general.

Indicators of Illness

When I speak about indicators of illness, I want to clarify that I am doing so in the context of a health reading. I am not suggesting that every time that these cards or patterns emerge, we are speaking about illness. I have querents who ask something like, "I have gone to the doctor multiple times, and they don't find anything wrong, but I am feeling bad/exhausted/in pain all the time. Do you see something wrong?"

I don't always or often see something wrong, but when I do, here is how it has presented itself to me.

A spread with a predominance of air is usually an indication that the issue may be somatic or a result of stress. However, a predominance of air with a Ten of Swords present has indicated more serious issues before, which were confirmed by the querent.

I am suspicious of The Moon in health-related readings, because it can be an indicator of a condition that is masked by something else, especially in readings that indicate that there is nothing technically wrong, but the querent still feels "off." The High Priestess works in a similar fashion, and the Seven of Swords seems to indicate that symptoms can be misleading with regards to the actual condition. All of this, of course, is dependent on if there is substantiation to determine that something is wrong.

Other frequent offenders are "balance" cards, such as the Two of Pentacles or Temperance, with some sort of ill aspect. This usually points to either an excess or deficit in the body that is behind the querent's symptoms. You may wonder what the point of this indicator might be if we don't have the power or the knowledge to fix it, but this kind of pointer might lead to a suggestion that the client can then follow up with their doctor. Perhaps the client has a food intolerance that isn't showing up on regular bloodwork, for example, and the reading points them in the right direction to investigate further. Of course, any advice given because of a tarot reading needs to be from a preventative perspective, solely considering options that do no harm to the querent.

I find the subject of health fascinating because it is, to me, the subject that varies the most on a case-by-case basis. It relies heavily on the context and the visual interpretation of the moment. A very interesting combination that I encountered once and that I look out for now was the Six of Cups with The Wheel of Fortune. This combination made me think about a potential comeback of a previously experienced condition. I have also seen the Ten of Pentacles speaking of inherited conditions, and there are other possibilities, such as The Magician and the Eight of Swords, that speak about an issue provoked by a work environment or one's routine. I have seen the Eight of Wands as an indicator of an allergic reaction.

If we turn to more serious conditions, I will say that I have very seldom run into indications of them unprompted. I have had very few of those occasions. When I have encountered them, rather than a set of cards or a particular pattern of elements, what I had was a gut feeling that accompanied the reading and that prompted me to recommend a health checkup to the querent. If there is something that concerns me in this aspect, I will say something that encourages the querent to see their healthcare provider in a way that doesn't sound fear-inducing, but that highlights the benefits of doing so.

I remember one case in which the cards revealed a combination that I didn't quite like. It was in a general reading that involved the Ace of Pentacles, The Devil, and The Moon in the inauspicious side of the queen card that represented my querent, and I told her not to skip her Pap smear. If I get something specific like that, I will say something along the lines of, "Look, it's probably nothing and I don't mean to induce any sort of panic here, but there are a couple of things here that make me think that you should get this checked, and since getting this checked can't hurt, I would rather say it and be wrong than not say it."

Reading on Complicated Health Matters

Readings in which the querent either is dealing with a diagnosed illness or is the caretaker of someone with one are very delicate in their nature. They require great care in their delivery and sensitivity on the part of the reader. Remember that if there are situations in which you feel uncomfortable reading, you need to respect your own boundaries.

In both cases, the querent's aim is usually towards management of the illness. These readings are usually not highly prediction oriented—and caretakers are often more interested in developments, understandably enough, than patients are—but rather oriented at managing expectations, conditions, and themselves, as well as the things they need to work through, emotionally speaking.

This is a very vulnerable type of reading, but also a beautiful one. They are beautiful because of the way they allow you to connect with another person, specifically a person who is going through something difficult and who is placing their trust in you as a reader.

My pointers here are more behavioral than reading oriented, though there are three main lines in which readings can develop: You can see indicators of decline, indicators of improvement, and pointers of manageability. That information is not necessarily for you to share, but for you to frame the reading.

Patterns of even numbers, balanced elements, and stable or cyclic cards are a sign of manageability. A proliferation of odd numbers and unbalanced elements may point towards a bout of a condition. Decline is probably the easiest to spot. It doesn't usually need a lot of identifying patterns. The cards will show it by themselves. Improvement is also usually shown pretty clearly.

In these situations, the querent does not want to know just about the illness itself, but also how to handle it on a personal and emotional level. You can use the techniques you've learned to provide the answers that they need.

Let's look at an example.

William is the main caretaker of his aunt Catherine. She is an elderly woman with the onset of dementia who is otherwise in good physical health. William is concerned about his ability to take care of his aunt as her illness progresses. He would like to plan for her future and is considering an assisted-living facility. He wants to know what the best moment to consider that transition would be.

There is something happening visually in the central column of this spread with Judgement, The Nine of Swords, and The Nine of Pentacles. This represents a very common experience for dementia patients, which is a difference in their cognition during the day versus at night. The fact that this is the central column suggests that this will be pivotal to William's decision.

I take it that, in his position as a caretaker, he is represented by the Knight of Wands in the reading, while Catherine is the Queen of Cups. The way that the Page of Swords and the Nine of Swords are right in front of her suggests that, at the point of the reading, she is aware that she is experiencing these symptoms, and she may be worried about her future. The Ace of Pentacles knighting the Queen of Cups and the Nine of Pentacles suggests that her otherwise good health is likely to outlast her awareness of the situation. It also suggests that she may have a plan herself or the means to provide for her future. The Queen of Cups knighting the Ace of Pentacles and the Eight of Wands with the Page of Swords in between them both may be confirmation that her mental decline will occur quicker than her physical one.

The knighting positions of the Knight of Wands being the Page of Swords and the Nine of Pentacles indicate that the decision will ultimately be William's to make and that he will have a way to cover it financially. However, the last column with the Knight of Wands, the Queen of Cups, and the Seven of Cups seems to point towards William and Catherine exploring options together. It will probably be best that they transition Catherine to an assisted living facility while she is still aware of herself and her surroundings during the day, in order to minimize confusion whenever possible.

End of Life

This is an extremely delicate issue, even more so than the ones that we have previously discussed. It is also a very controversial subject. There are more than a few readers who refuse to consider dealing with death in their readings.

My take is that if tarot is the book of life, then it is not possible that it doesn't also deal with one of the most universal experiences that everyone and everything will face sooner or later. This does not mean that we should predict death left and right, nor does it mean that you need to include it in your readings if you don't feel comfortable with it.

Now, when I speak about predicting death, I don't speak about asking the cards when your terrible mother-in-law will die, nor am I saying that you need to even get into a specific "when" someone might die. But there are circumstances in which reading on the end-of-life can be useful and helpful.

The people that have asked me about end-of-life questions the most have been caretakers and family members of people who were diagnosed with a terminal illness. Being a caretaker in such conditions is an incredibly difficult and all-consuming task, even when it is done with the utmost love, and I would never judge someone for wanting to know what to expect in this sort of situation.

I have also worked with people who needed to plan around these situations and make decisions. Once I had a querent who had a dream job interview. This interview was the culmination of a decade of work, but they had to fly out of the country for it. At the same time, the querent's father was in the last expected weeks of his life. They wanted to know if they had time to make that trip and return while they still had time with their father. The answer I divined to that question was a "no," which ended up being correct. The querent was glad to have avoided, in their own words, a lifetime of regret as a result of that reading.

What do you look out for as a reader to confirm such an event? Careful! Be mindful when reading this section. I am by no means suggesting that every time you see one of these cards, combinations, or patterns, that it is speaking about someone's passing!

There are so many different answers to this question. I have seen death very few times, but when I have seen it, it's been in very different ways. If a person has been diagnosed with a terminal illness and suddenly there is a disruption in the spread that leads to very positive cards, it can speak of the release after a long period of suffering. There is no need for the Death card to appear in the spread for it to indicate a death.

The Death card may sometimes be present, but not necessarily. I have a few cards that, in different combinations, have appeared around matters of death: The Chariot, Death, The Sun, Judgement, The World, Ace of Swords, Four of Swords, Six of Swords, and Ten of Swords. Readings in which the earth element is missing may also speak about the end of material life.

Thoughts on Reading for Health

I encourage you to be open to considering different possibilities about reading for the often heavy and complicated matters surrounding health. Consider for yourself how it may be useful to accompany our querents when they are dealing with such complicated situations, whether they are personally experiencing them or they are a caretaker for someone else. These are some of the toughest experiences a reader can have, but also some of the deepest.

Chapter 16

Reading for Spiritual Purposes

The spiritual path is unique to each of us who walk it, and I am of the belief that nobody can communicate with your spiritual court better than you yourself, nor will anyone be able to tell you what is right for your spiritual development better than you.

However, sometimes we all may feel the need to outsource our spiritual guidance, and it is our job as readers to be able to respond to that need for our clients, and, of course, for ourselves too. We may encounter situations in which we need to confirm or validate a perception, feel stuck in our spiritual practice, or need to find a way forward.

It is not uncommon to also deal with the big questions. Querents can get very creative with their deep questions, ranging from "What is my life's purpose?" to "What is the purpose of humanity in the big picture?" Yeah, good luck with that one!

The diversity of spiritual questions is too ample to treat in this or probably any one book. This is one of those areas where you have to be creative with your skills, and pray to your gods (pun intended).

Aside from the wide variety of spiritual questions that you can expect, our querents might also have unrealistic expectations regarding our abilities. It is not uncommon to find a querent that believes that a tarot reader and a medium are always the same thing, or that you have a direct line with their guides. For this reason, I encourage you to set realistic expectations about what your querent can and cannot expect from the session.

That said, if you have worked through your core meanings, and you get the hang of reading contextually, you can still get quite a few answers for your querent. You can even be an interpreter of messages from the other side, if not directly then through your cards.

Reading about Spiritual Messages

When reading about spiritual messages, whether from the querent's spiritual team, ancestors, or whomever they request a message from, the first thing that I do is inform them that I am just an interpreter of cards and I am not a medium. The second thing that I do is rely a lot on symbolism. There's a specific exercise that I recommend to help readers who are not mediums translate spiritual messages with the help of tarot, and it is this game.

Pick a deck of cards and, using them as your only language, choose the cards that you would use to explain to someone who doesn't read tarot what you do for a living. If you happen to be a lawyer, you could pull Justice and call it a day, but if you are a carpenter, you might choose the Eight of Pentacles and the Ace of Wands and pray that the person makes the connection that it means working + wood. Think of it a little like charades, just with tarot cards.

When we are transmitting messages, we sometimes have to be very literal with symbols. Sometimes, the symbol is about the card meaning, but it might also be about what is happening in the card, what is drawn on it, or about a specific figure's posture. What is clear is that, if you want to succeed, the best way is by thinking out of the box and beyond the traditional interpretation.

I will give you an example from my own notes. When doing ancestor work, I pulled a Court Card to find the ancestor that was willing to step up and work with me throughout it. I pulled the Knight of Cups of the *Bohemian Gothic Tarot* by Baba Studios (an absolutely gorgeous deck, by the way). This depiction of the Knight of Cups showcases a figure that doesn't look very gentle, contrary to other examples of the card that we can find. He's holding a cup in his hand; however, the gesture is somewhat aggressive, as if he is ready to hit someone with it without a second thought. This made me think of a particular ancestor who was known for being an alcoholic. I noticed a few other things: The knight is wearing a metallic helmet, and the shape of the cup reminded me of a grenade. These two details made me think of an ancestor who passed away in an explosion. I was torn between those two ancestors that first came to mind, but then I noticed a symbol that tilted the scale: A fleur de lis.

The crest of my second surname, Hernando (in Spain we have two surnames), contains multiple fleur de lis, and that detail was the one that made me understand that the card was referring to the ancestor who was known for not being too kind and having a taste for drink.

That is an example of how personal and significant symbolism can be in this kind of reading.

"Which Deity Should I Work With?" Readings

While oddly specific, this is a reading that I have been requested enough times to feel that it deserves its own mention. There may be situations when a querent comes to you for help in working with a spiritual deity. It may be that they feel a certain spiritual calling, but they are unsure where it is coming from, or they may feel stuck in their spiritual practice and require assistance determining what deity would best suit their needs. There are a few cards in tarot that are associated with particular deities, such Mercury/Hermes for The Magician, Venus/Aphrodite for The Empress, Mars/Ares for The Emperor, Odin/Kronos for The Hermit, or Diana/Selene for The Moon, just to name a few.

But what do we do when a client is asking what deity the cards recommend for their spiritual practice? More than simply finding a particular deity as represented by a specific card, what I like to do is work with a descriptive reading to find information about what this recommended deity is like, and what information is available about working with them. I will then see if it matches the call that the querent is receiving.

Another option when a querent is interested in working with a new or unknown deity is to try to deduce the deity's mythology through the reading. The Nine Card Tableau can be useful for this. It gives you a core that reflects the "main thing" for the deity. This may their main challenge or what they represent, as well as a story to explore. Myths are often similar among different cultures, so even if you reach one conclusion based on your own cultural background, it can end up representing something else for your querent.

Let's see an example (page 194).

I like a few things in this reading very much. The Page of Pentacles is right at the core of the spread. It provides the feeling of a student who is ready to begin learning. This seems to confirm that the querent is indeed about to begin developing a spiritual path.

I also like that The Fool and The World are in the same row. This takes us on a journey from one end of the Major Arcana to the other, which indicates the querent's spiritual development. The Six of Swords in the middle only strengthens this interpretation, bringing forward motion. The Page of Pentacles sitting between the Ace of Wands and the Two of Pentacles turns that call the querent feels into a spiritual relationship.

Based on this reading, we can conclude that the querent is being called or is about to start a spiritual connection. One question remains: with whom?

We have the King of Swords present in the spread, which brings a masculine deity into the reading. Maybe this is because I am a big-time Greek mythology nerd, but when I saw the King of Swords, the King of Cups, and The Devil, I thought to myself, "The king of the sky, the king of the sea, and the king of the underworld." To me, this is a reference to Zeus, Poseidon, and Hades.

Which of the three, though, is the one our querent should work with, if the clue was that line of thought?

Looking at the positions and knightings of the three, I would say that there is no wrong choice. They all are equally close to the querent and they all seem to bring opportunities. However, with that being said, the King of Swords is the one that to me holds the most weight in this reading. There are a few reasons for this. First, it is in the nuance position. It knights the Two of Cups and the Six of Swords, which reinforces that idea of establishing a relationship and beginning a journey. The King of Swords, Ace of Wands, and The Fool forming a column seems to confirm that opening or that opportunity in a more direct way.

Now, does this mean that the deity has to be Zeus? Not necessarily. My point of view is that this information was presented to me in a way that I could understand so that I could transmit the message. When explaining this to the querent, I would say something like, "This is the conclusion I am receiving, but my interpretation is based on my experience. Have you been thinking about a deity with similar mythology or a similar position within their pantheon as this deity?" From there, you can help the querent figure out what makes the most sense for them.

Reading for spiritual matters can be challenging in the sense that it puts your interpretative skills to the test, but it's also one of the areas that makes you think out of the box the most, which is immensely helpful to hone your skills as a reader. It's also an aspect that you can practice with yourself, and a reading style that can be conversational and enriching on both ends.

Concluding Thoughts

If you have made it this far, you must have a very solid foundation in the tableau system by now. You might have done a first reading with the idea of going back to practice later, or you might have taken it one step at a time and paused in between chapters to fully grasp the material. Either way, it is my sincere hope that you have learned something that you can take with you in your future as a tarot reader.

Crediting the tableau with having changed my life might seem like an exaggeration, but I know that it did not only once, but three times.

The first time was when I discovered what would become my Nine Card Tableau, that version of a layered reading in a narrow rectangle of twelve that gave me insight into a pretty lousy relationship and that made me more confident in my interpretative skills.

The second time, many years later, was when I found out that the Nine Card Tableau was far from my own creation, and that it was actually a whole system with a backstory. It felt quite serendipitous, and it gave me a great deal of reassurance in my reading skills, as well as shaping my style as a reader.

My career as a diviner has been defined by the tableau. It is how I read, and it is what I teach.

The third time that the tableau changed my life was when I met my very first student, or my very first padawan, as I call them. (I like to make a nerdy reference to *Star Wars.*) If you have enjoyed this book, take a moment to thank Leslie, the best padawan one could ever dream of, because without her, these pages would simply not be in your hands. How did the tableau change my life for the third time? When I first met Leslie, she became fascinated by the system, and she convinced me of two things: First, that I was a good teacher. Second, that the tableau was, as they say, "the best thing since sliced bread," and that I needed to spread the word about the system far and wide. She had so much faith in this that she wrote the table of contents for this book in late 2020, if I recall correctly, when she began to insist that I needed to write it.

It sat patiently in a Google Doc for four more years, until the opportunity to make it a reality arose. The tableau has given me many things, and her belief in me has probably been the best of them all. I have taught the tableau to students from all around the globe since, and I always carry a little bit of Leslie with me when I do it.

Maybe the tableau has a fourth surprise in store now that it has become that book that was dreamt of, when it reaches your hands, and you too become fascinated by the richness and reliability of the method. I get excited when I think about the new students that it will reach!

Happy reading!

Recommended Reading

21 Ways to Read a Tarot Card by Mary K. Greer, Llewellyn Publications, 2006

Archetypal Tarot by Mary K. Greer, Weiser Books, 2021

Fortune Stellar by Christiana Gaudet, Cards and Crafts Inc., 2017

Magical Tarot by Madame Pamita, Weiser Books, 2023

The New Tarot Handbook by Rachel Pollack, Llewellyn Publications, 2012

Phantasmagoria (Companion book to *The Tarot of Vampyres*), by Ian Daniels, Llewellyn Publications, 2017

The Psychic Art of Tarot by Mat Auryn, Llewellyn Publications, 2024

Seventy-Eight Degrees of Wisdom by Rachel Pollack, Weiser Books, 2019

Tarot for Your Self by Mary K. Greer, Weiser Books, 2019

Tarot Interactions by Deborah Lipp, Llewellyn Publications, 2015

Tarot: No Questions Asked by Theresa Reed, Weiser Books, 2020

Tarot on Earth by Tom Benjamin, (pub. by author), 2017

Tarot Tour Guide by Christiana Gaudet, Card and Craft Inc., 2012

Untold Tarot by Caitlín Matthews, RedFeather, 2018

A Walk through the Forest of Souls by Rachel Pollack, Weiser Books, 2023

Your Tarot Toolkit by Tom Benjamin, (pub. by author), 2021

About the Author

María Alviz Hernando is a tarot reader, divination teacher, author, deck creator, and international speaker. Her signature style, known as tarot tableau, blends traditional tarot and European cartomancy techniques, resulting in a system that aims to make tarot effective, useful, and to the point. As a reader, she combines a predictive approach with practical analysis, exploring the possibilities available and offering actionable steps to deal with matters that are truly important to her querents.

As one of the directors of the World Divination Association, María is dedicated to promoting the love for divination worldwide. Education is a cornerstone of María's work including diverse forms of divination training and personal mentoring. María has had the privilege of presenting at numerous online and in-person conferences, including the WDA Big Bang Conference, Lenormand Summit, Divination Pride, Stockholm Tarot Conference, WDA Virtual Conference, Staar and the TABI Summer Conference. She lives in Madrid, Spain. Find Maria at *thesibylstarot.com*.

To Our Readers

Weiser Books, an imprint of Red Wheel/Weiser, publishes books across the entire spectrum of occult, esoteric, speculative, and New Age subjects. Our mission is to publish quality books that will make a difference in people's lives without advocating any one particular path or field of study. We value the integrity, originality, and depth of knowledge of our authors.

Our readers are our most important resource, and we appreciate your input, suggestions, and ideas about what you would like to see published.

Visit our website at *www.redwheelweiser.com,* where you can learn about our upcoming books and free downloads, and also find links to sign up for our newsletter and exclusive offers.

You can also contact us at *info@rwwbooks.com* or at

Red Wheel/Weiser, LLC
65 Parker Street, Suite 7
Newburyport, MA 01950

Also by Mark Critch

Son of a Critch:
A Childish Newfoundland Memoir

An Embarrassment of Critch's:
Immature Stories from My Grown-Up Life

Sorry,
Not Sorry